MIND = BLOWN

MIND=
BLOWN

Amazing Facts About This Weird,
Hilarious, Insane World

MATTHEW SANTORO
WITH JAKE GREENE

Illustrations by Kagan McLeod

PENGUIN

an imprint of Penguin Canada, a division of
Penguin Random House Canada Limited

Canada • USA • UK • Ireland • Australia • New Zealand • India •
South Africa • China

Published in Penguin paperback by Penguin Canada, 2016

Simultaneously published in the United States by TarcherPerigee,
an imprint of Penguin Random House LLC

www.penguinrandomhouse.ca

LIBRARY AND ARCHIVES CANADA CATALOGUING IN PUBLICATION

Santoro, Matthew, author
Mind=blown / Matthew Santoro and Jake Greene.

ISBN 978-0-14-319811-6 (paperback)
ISBN 978-0-14-319812-3 (electronic)

1. Curiosities and wonders--Humor. I. Greene, Jake,
author II. Title.

AG243.S25 2016   031.02   C2015-906657-3

Book design by Katy Riegel
Cover design by Matt Vee
Cover image by Matthew Santoro

Printed and bound in the United States of America

10 9 8 7 6 5 4 3 2 1

CONTENTS

PART 5:
Fact Favorites

INTRODUCTION

Six Septembers

SIX YEARS, HUNDREDS of videos, and thousands of facts ago, I uploaded my first video to YouTube. That first post was called "Text the Pope!" because I talked about how weird it was that the Vatican had just launched a service allowing people to send text messages to His Holiness. I also shared a few weird tidbits about my life, cut away to a *Sesame Street* mash-up clip, introduced a clone, and complained that I couldn't get Usher's smash hit "OMG" out of my head. "Text the Pope!" was random, frantic, and weirdly orange (I didn't know about color correction back then). For all of the video's shortcomings, however, I have never thought about pulling it down from YouTube. I am really proud of that first video, not so much for the content in it but for the act of putting it out into the world.

Throughout most of high school and college, I was a really conservative guy. I didn't take risks and I didn't chase dreams.

My first YouTube video was a representation of my desire to change both of those things. When I started making videos, I didn't know a single thing about production, but I knew I wanted to learn more about the world and I wanted to share more of myself with the world. When I uploaded "Text the Pope!" I had no idea where YouTube would take me, but I was committing to the journey.

While looking back through some of my early efforts, I noticed an interesting pattern. I seem to experience a lot of pivotal life events and epiphanies in September. As I scrolled my way down memory lane I couldn't help but laugh at the marked moments of evolution and growth that took place during that month. In fact, my vlogs and videos from the past six Septembers perfectly lay out the chronology of my YouTube story, and so I want to share pieces of those September posts so that you can better understand not only the path that I've traveled but also how I was feeling along the way.

September 2010: "Who I Am NOT & Auto-Tune!"

"Hey, I know you! You're that guy in that show!"

When you search for direction and passion in life, it's much easier to identify who you don't want to be than who you dream of becoming, which is why it's so interesting to me that one of my September 2010 vlogs was partially titled "Who I Am NOT." In the video, I talk about random people on the street mistaking me for celebrities to whom I bear a slight resemblance—Bruce Willis, Mr. Clean, Jason Statham, and other famous bald guys. What's funny here is that people were straining to figure out who I was on the street while I was straining to figure out who I was in my videos.

Auto-Tune, meanwhile, was in the news at the time because T-Pain (the hip-hop artist) was trying to patent its use in popular music. Artists use Auto-Tune to make their voices sound like everyone else's, which in a sense is what I was doing on my channel in 2010. I had discovered a lot of the early YouTube stars such as Ray William Johnson, Dan Brown, Philip DeFranco, Meekakitty, WheezyWaiter, and others, and I was really entertained and amazed by what they did (and the attention they were getting). The influence of those pioneering YouTubers is clearly evident in my early videos as I frequently experimented with their formats and structures.

Back in 2010 I never thought that I could make YouTube my full-time job. It was just an outlet that allowed me to continue to be a goofball in life. Making videos kept me sane and awake while I was fighting off sleep and looking at people's taxes at the accounting firm where I worked.

September 2011: "YouTube Full-Time??"

"Video production is my real passion. Right now it's a hobby but I would love for it one day to be my full-time job. . . . That's kind of the dream, right?"

One of the things I love about the "YouTube Full-Time??" vlog entry is my obvious paranoia that people from my accounting firm were watching my videos. I was clearly more excited about videos and social media than I was about work but I had to tone down my enthusiasm on camera so that I wouldn't risk jeopardizing my employment. At one point in the video, I caught myself openly fantasizing about a life in video production and then felt compelled to quickly throw in "I love my job! I have a great job and it's a great place to work!" as though someone was going to rat me out to my boss if I was too honest. That said, my favorite part about the "YouTube Full-Time??" vlog post is that, looking back, I can clearly see how important my fans were becoming in my life, let alone on my channel. I say this a lot, but I view my fans as an extension of my family and I seek their/your help in overcoming obstacles or answering tough questions that pop up in my life. In that September 2011 vlog post, I didn't know if I was ready to pursue a career in videos, so I asked my (albeit small at the time) fan family. *"I could do YouTube full-time. So, that's kind of my dream and I'm not really sure if I should do it or not and I thought I'd throw that by you guys."* The comments, e-mails, and support I received from fans in those first couple of years really helped me keep my eyes on the prize, even though my view counts weren't spectacular and I was still a couple of years away from blowing up.

September 2012: "I Lost My Job Today"

"I think this is life's way of telling me that maybe I should go into film production. There's sort of a sense of calm, of freedom. Even though I'm at the bottom right now, my life is completely open. As silly as that may sound, it's really freeing. Sometimes life forces you to take steps towards a path that you were meant to go on."

Getting fired from my accounting job was the single best thing that could've happened for my career. Losing my job forced me to wake up and confront my true feelings about what I wanted to do with my life. Looking back, I think, "Gosh, what took me so long?" but you know what? It's hard to make a change after committing yourself to five years of school (and debt) and staring down societal expectations.

For the next two years, I was happy and broke. I started shooting weddings to make ends meet, and I scrapped for other work, but I stayed committed to my YouTube channel and I really began to develop my voice. I started posting infotainment lists and I was really excited about the learning and teaching I was able to do as a result of researching my weekly topics and facts. I injected comedy into each video because I didn't want to lose my goofball energy, but the real excitement came from sharing my love of learning.

September 2013: "Exciting Things Are Happening!"

"It's amazing how if you stick with something long enough and really believe in yourself and work hard . . . then it really does pay off. . . . Some really amazing things are happening."

When I posted the "Exciting Things Are Happening!" video, I had just jumped from 25,000 subscribers to 30,000 in a week. Little did I know that between September 2013 and May 2014, I would go from 30,000 subscribers to 1,000,000! Then, from May 2014 through July 2014, my subscriber base would double to 2,000,000! There was a three-month period in there when I was literally getting tens of thousands of subscribers a day. And here's the best part about it: *I achieved all the growth without going viral.* What I mean by that is that I didn't have one single video that grabbed tens of millions of hits. Instead all of my videos were growing quickly and steadily, meaning I wasn't in danger of becoming a one-hit wonder. Earlier in 2013, I had partnered with a multichannel network, Collective Digital Studio (now Studio 71), and they helped prepare me for success. They also began to broker the collaboration opportunities with other YouTubers that would help me grow even more in 2013 and 2014.

September 2014: "So Close to the Finish Line . . ."

"I feel like I'm in the end of a race. I'm in a marathon and I can see the finish line . . . but I'm losing steam. . . . I can't give up now. I'm so close."

By September 2014, I was starting to achieve my dreams, but it was completely exhausting. I was getting a million views a week and I could hardly believe it because I was still the same guy who was excited about getting two thousand views the previous year. I shot "So Close to the Finish Line . . ." right before my first blockbuster collaboration tour through Los Angeles, the trip that would establish me as a contemporary with some of my longtime YouTube heroes, like the Fine Brothers and Rhett & Link. The year that followed was amazing and exhausting and it went by in an instant. It seemed like I was achieving everything I had set out to do, which meant that it was time for me to innovate, reinvent, and expand my horizons.

September 2015: "I Won a Streamy Award!!"

I want to say thank you to everyone because you continue to support me through so much and I honestly believe that my audience is unique. . . . I genuinely feel like you're all my friends, like you're part of my extended family. Truthfully, you guys do as much for me in making my dreams a reality as anyone in my life. All I can say is thank you. I am humbled and I'm honored that I get to do what I do for you on a daily basis. My goodness. I'm just incredibly happy and excited. . . . In September 2015, I made a vlog putting out into the universe that I'm happy, putting it out there that I'm thankful and I'm grateful. And look what happened that very night. I won a Streamy Award (for "Breakout Creator"). You manifest what you want to happen. If you put good things into the world, good things will come to you. . . . It changes your life when you start thinking positively and put good things into the universe.

What a ride. My mind = blown.

THE PURPOSE OF
MIND = BLOWN

(Enjoy + Learn + Share) x Life

THERE ISN'T A single definition for the phrase "blow your mind" because every mind is different and is therefore amazed by different information and experiences. In the *Historical Dictionary of the 1960s*, James Stuart Olson tells us that hippies first began using the term "blow your mind" as a way to express a "sense of being absolutely overwhelmed by a new idea or new perception."[1] The website urbandictionary.com offers a few separate user-generated definitions for *blow your mind*, ranging from the simple "to be amazed by something amazing" to the expressive "It's like, you know, so far out that it's in, and so like, in, you know, that it's so far out! Can you dig it? Like, it's so hot that it's cool, and it's so cool that it's hot! It like makes you like to say like. I mean, try it, you'll like it, man!"[2] I like that definition best because it's the most fun to read out loud.

A simple YouTube search will reveal that there are count-less music videos for songs with some version of "blow your mind" in the title and each video is a crazy different interpre-tation of the phrase. Eve and Gwen Stefani ride four-wheelers to a swanky black tie party in their "Let Me Blow Ya Mind" video, while the video for "Blow Your Mind" by Tiësto & MOTi tells the story of a loser who crashes a lawn bowling tourna-ment at a European senior citizens home and ends up getting his butt kicked by two ruthless old ladies who pour iced tea all over his white clothes after repeatedly whacking him with their purses. In the Bollywood dance hit "Mind Blowing Ma-hiya," Indian music superstar Sunidhi Chauhan takes over a seaside city by laying siege via large-group booty-shaking Bollywood dance numbers.

Fun fact: Sunidhi Chauhan is one of India's most popular "playback singers," which means that she records songs spe-cifically for movie soundtracks that the stars of the movie lip-sync during on-screen musical numbers. According to Wikipedia, playback singer Lata Mangeshkar was credited by the *Guinness World Records* for having sung more than thirty thousand solo, duet, and chorus-backed recordings, more than any other singer in the world at the time. What's even more mind blowing, however, is that twenty years later, in 2011, the *Guinness World Records* title for "Most Recorded Artist in History" was given to Mangeshkar's sister, Asha Bhosle.[3] Apparently Asha and Lata grew up in a pretty com-petitive household.

What was I talking about again? Right, the book!

Whether you are interested in Bollywood, Baltimore, or

Mordor, I hope the crazy facts in this book blow your mind and I hope you share your favorites with your friends. I want you to use this book to spread your love of learning and to stimulate fun conversations as well as your imagination.

In addition to blowing your mind, this book will prepare you for life! After reading everything here you will be completely prepared to:

- **Dominate Weddings and Happy Hours**—When the rest of the room resorts to discussing the weather or begging the bartender to turn on the game, you will amaze the after-work or cocktail crowd with your knowledge of rogue planets, secret Russian prisons, and why Chinese superstitions suggest that the mother of the bride shouldn't be wearing her favorite green hat during the ceremony (spoiler: It's a symbol of adultery!).

- **Nail Your Job Interviews**—There comes a point in the hiring process when your potential boss will look across her or his desk and think: "This person has the right résumé and references—but will she or he be an interesting person to have around every day?" This is when you start talking about advancements in artificial intelligence, or perhaps you can show your future mentor that you have advanced critical-thinking skills by making the argument that Bruce Willis and American general Douglas MacArthur are real-world doppelgängers.

- **Astound Small Children**—Watch their little eyes go wide when you recount the heroic tale of LuLu the Vietnamese potbellied pig, who saved her owner's life by flagging down passing cars. You should also prepare for an onslaught of questions about the gray magic of Marie Laveau, the voodoo queen of New Orleans, or about how Frank Epperson invented Popsicles when he was only eleven years old!

▪ **Wow Your Future In-laws**—Deflect awkward or critical questions about your relationship by talking about how young Polish men and women get pussy (willow) whipped on Dyngus Day. Or you could tell Mom and Dad about how their daughter's smile knocks you out like .01 gram of etorphine (without the deadly side effects).

▪ **Uncover a New Passion**—My dream is that while reading this book, you will be inspired to learn more about ancient Egypt, penguins that wear backpacks, the Secret Service, the Shin-Kicking World Championships, or anything else that ignites your own love of learning and compels you to share your findings with the world both online and off-line.

But wait, there's more!

When I set out to write this book, not only did I want to share my own love of learning with the world, but I also wanted to celebrate my creative and passionate friends and fans, which is why I asked them to send me their favorite facts for inclusion in this book as well. Within forty-eight hours of posting my video request, my in-box was overflowing with amazing facts from around the globe!

Did you know that bald men around the world are 13 percent more powerful than men with hair?[4] Well, thanks to Alex Aberdein from Ontario, Canada, you do now!

In addition to the Fan Facts sprinkled throughout the chapters of this book, there is an entire "Fan Fact Favorites" section at the end. Since my fans are the reason that I'm in a position to write a book in the first place, it only seemed right to get them involved in the creative process.

Okay, enough with the setup. I hope this book blows your mind.

Part 1

RULES OF AMAZEMENT

QUADRILLION-DOLLAR COWS

(And Other Crazy Facts About Money)

PEOPLE DO CRAZY things for money, and throughout history, they have also used crazy things *as* money. Cows, stones, and gold coins that weigh a hundred kilograms have all served as currency. Naturally, as soon as a new form of money pops into circulation, a new form of criminal will begin trying to knock it off (with the exception of cows; I couldn't find any historical references to criminals trying to pass fake cows as cash). Bottom line: For thousands of years, money has made the world go round and made people go nuts.

Cows are the oldest currency in the world.[1] Cows were domesticated in roughly 9000 BC and people began using them as currency almost immediately. In fact, in parts of Africa, cows are still used as money. A couple of years ago, a South African software developer created a firestorm when he developed an app to assess a woman's *lobola*, or "bride price," as a combination of cash and cattle. According to that app, a twenty-five-year-old woman with a job who considers herself to be "very beautiful" and has both children and a high school certificate would command a price of "$500 and no cows" on the marital market. After being (appropriately) perceived as offensive, sexist, and degrading to women, the app was updated to include a groom price as well. Classy move.

The oldest bank still in operation today isn't exactly a "mountain of piety."[2] The Monte di Pietà was founded in 1472 in what was then the Republic of Siena. In 1624 when the bank was incorporated into Tuscany, it was given its current name, Banca Monte dei Paschi di Siena. The bank's beautiful headquarters in Siena look like the perfect setting for a Hollywood heist movie; in fact, the building has seen its fair share of high-level drama and scandal over the years. In 2013, it was revealed that mismanagement, fraud, poor investments, and misinformation had left the bank in financial ruin and in need of a bailout. As I write this, the Monte dei Paschi di Siena's future is still up in the air.

The U.S. Secret Service protects more money than Presidents.[3] According to secretservice.gov, the U.S. Secret Service, the organization we most often associate with protecting the personal safety of the President of the United States, "was created on July 5, 1865 in Washington, D.C., to suppress counterfeit currency." At the time, it was estimated that at least a third of the currency in circulation in the country was fake. The Secret Service didn't begin to take on presidential protection until 1902—which is too bad because, ironically, President Lincoln was assassinated by John Wilkes Booth the day

Lincoln established the Secret Service. For the past 115 years, the Secret Service has continued to investigate fraud while also ensuring the safety of foreign and domestic diplomats. From 2003 to 2008, the organization made nearly 29,000 arrests for counterfeiting, cybercrime, and financial crimes, and seized nearly $300 million in counterfeit currency, while preventing nearly $12 billion in losses. Guess that means protecting the president's backside is actually their side gig.

A Tale of Two Counterfeiters: Old School[4] and Bold School[5]

In 1938, some funny money started turning up around Manhattan. The counterfeit bills were unique for a few different reasons: They were very poorly executed, they were used infrequently (no more than fifty per month), and they were all one-dollar bills. Most counterfeiters during that time (and most other times) favored larger bills. After all, if you were going to risk imprisonment, conventional wisdom said that you might want to manufacture more than just petty cash. The other confusing aspect to this counterfeit case was that the bills were never used at the same location twice. Authorities were baffled. Who was this crazy counterfeiter? For ten years, the Secret Service hunted for this one-dollar bandit, referring to him by his case number as "Mr. 880."

As it turns out, Mr. 880 was an old widower named Edward Mueller. Mr. Mueller had spent most of his life as an average Joe, but when his wife passed away something inside him snapped. He quit his job, became a junk collector, and then started printing the extra cash when he realized that his new profession wouldn't exactly pay the bills for him and his dog.

The manhunt for Mr. 880 was frustrating both financially and morally for the Secret Service. Every time one of his fake bills showed up, agents would be dispatched to the business where the cash was passed. The agents would then take great pains to educate the shopkeepers on what to look for when trying to spot fake currency. However, because Mueller never hit the same joint twice, the training was a waste of time. Mr. 880 was finally caught in 1945 at the age of seventy-three. He was sentenced to a year in jail but his sentence was eventually reduced to four months. A movie about him was made in 1950 called *Mister 880*, starring Burt Lancaster. Mueller made more money from that movie than he did during his entire counterfeiting career.

Now, if Mueller's four-month prison sentence seems a little bit light, wait until you read about this next guy. . . .

Frank Bourassa was a small-time Canadian drug dealer and former car thief when he began making counterfeit U.S. twenty-dollar bills in the late 2000s. Funnily enough, Bourassa learned exactly what features he needed to include in his fake bills by studying U.S. government websites. He struck a deal with a European paper mill for the perfect stock by convincing them he was making twenty-dollar bonds. Armed with materials and knowledge, Bourassa then printed $250 million in U.S. twenties and began selling them to overseas buyers at thirty cents on the dollar. Eventually, he sold to an undercover agent and was arrested for counterfeiting in 2014. But that's when Bourassa's story really gets interesting. Upon arresting Bourassa at his house, police found roughly a million dollars in counterfeit bills. Over the next couple of months, as Canadian and U.S. forces searched for more fake cash, Bourassa struck a deal with his prosecutors: He would turn over an additional $200 million if they agreed to let him off with time served. In the end, the prospect of keeping the fake $200 million out of circulation was too good to pass up and the authorities let Bourassa go free. Thus, one of the most prolific counterfeiters in history now works as a consultant and life coach, offering services that range from "brand protection and fraud shielding" to "shattering the limits of possibilities" on his website, mastercounterfeiter.com.

The biggest coins in the world come from the island of Yap.[6] One type of currency that is in no danger of being knocked off is the rai stones from the Dr. Seuss–sounding island of Yap. In fact, I am going to tell you about the stones as though I were Dr. Seuss.

Long ago the island of Yap had no money.
Transactions were confusing and not at all funny.

Then explorers arrived with limestone from afar
that was carved into disks, some as large as your car.

They were called the rai stones.
All the locals approved.
But they were quite tough to trade for they couldn't be moved.

So the people kept track of the stones that they owned.
They passed small ones around, left the large ones alone.

The system made sense.
It wasn't so hard.
You could spend money that sat in my yard.

Okay, that's enough Seuss for now. The Bank of Canada in Ottawa actually has one of the large rai stones on display in its lobby. I wonder how many customers think the stone is actually a prehistoric hockey puck. . . .

FAN FACT: If you spin a penny ten thousand times, it won't land on heads 50 percent of the time. The heads picture actually weighs more than the tails image, so it ends up on the bottom more often.[7]

—*Russell F., Troy, N.Y.*

The **$10,000 bill is still legal in the United States (if you can find one).**[8] In 1928 and 1934, the U.S. Treasury printed roughly fifty thousand $10K notes. Of those, roughly 330 have survived deterioration and destruction. The large notes feature Abraham Lincoln's secretary of the treasury, Salmon P. Chase, the man who introduced paper currency into the economy during the Civil War. (A few fun facts about Chase: He was the governor of Ohio, a senator, the secretary of the treasury, and the chief justice of the Supreme Court. Also, he was married three times and each of his wives died young. Hmmm . . .) Of the 330 bills left in circulation, 100 of them were part of a wall display that hung in the Horseshoe casino in downtown Las Vegas for forty-five years, until that display was sold to a private collector in 2000. Asked why the display was taken down, casino ownership stated: "People are not as impressed about a million dollars as they used to be. When it first went up, it was like looking at a billion dollars."[9]

A $10,000 bill is nothing compared to Canada's $1,000,000 coin.[10] In 2007, the Royal Canadian Mint made a handful of 99.999 percent pure gold coins, worth $1,000,000 and weighing 100 kg each. At the time, they were the first million-dollar coins ever made. One side of the massive coin features Queen Elizabeth II, while the reverse side is adorned with a hand-polished maple leaf. Initially, only five of these coins were made and they were all immediately snatched up by jewelers and collectors for an average price of roughly $2,300,000. Scarcity certainly does drive up the price. In fact, when contacted by Canadian press, one of the first buyers, a jeweler in Vancouver, revealed that he had quickly "flipped" the coin at a significant premium to one of his investors. What does one do with a 100 kg coin? Mount it on the wall? Make a coffee table out of it? Build a bank to keep it in or, better yet, a giant cash register?

Zimbabwe once had a $100,000,000,000,000 bill.[12] In
2009, Zimbabwe introduced a *one-hundred-trillion*-dollar bank
note. However, before you envision a well-dressed African ty-
coon using one of these bills to buy entire continents in cash,
keep in mind that the value of the $100,000,000,000,000 bill
was only about thirty American dollars. The massive notes
came about as a result of hyperinflation during a period of
economic instability and transition that began in the 1990s
and continued until the country phased out their own currency in favor of the U.S. dollar in 2015. By June 2015, the
Zimbabwe dollar was so worthless that it could be exchanged
at a rate of thirty-five quadrillion dollars to one U.S. dollar,
which means that for nearly a year the country was full of
quadrillion-dollar cows.

BONUS FACTS!

- Instead of GNP, Bhutan measures growth and prosperity
  by gross national happiness. It has been doing this since
  1971.[13]
- Famous celebrities often use ink as currency.[14] Marlon
  Brando didn't like to sign autographs, which is why his
  personal checks are worth far more than the amounts of

money for which they are written. The artist Salvador Dalí used to draw on his checks as a way of getting out of paying for dinner. He knew his artsy doodles would be more valuable than the cost of his meal and the checks would never be cashed.

RULES OF AMAZEMENT

Crazy Laws from History and Beyond

I COULD FILL an entire book with crazy laws from around the world. One chapter could compare the age children can get married with the age they are allowed to drink beer. Another section could focus entirely on laws governing the ownership of and interaction with pets (because some countries get weird when it comes to puppy love). I could cover hypocritical laws, hippopotamus laws, and hip-replacement laws. However, as you are likely aware, I am not a lawyer. I am but a simple former Canadian accountant with an attention span incapable of supporting an entire book on a single topic. Therefore, rather than curating an entire catalogue of laws, I will present to you an album of the globe's greatest legal hits and misses.

The Ancient Extremists

In medieval Japan, samurai could kill peasants in order to test a new sword or fighting style.[1] This is reason number one million why it sucked to be a peasant in medieval Japan. Can you imagine? You're walking home from a fifteen-hour day of farming someone else's land when a samurai approaches you on the road:

"What's up, Steve?"

"Not much, Gary. Oh, hey, I got a new sword."

"Cool. Can I see it?"

"Yeah, man. I think I might actually test it on your face."

"Oh. That sucks. But, hey, what can I do, right? It's the law."

"Sure is. Now pretend like you're an enemy attacker. . . ."

The practice was called *tsujigiri*, which translates to "crossroads killing," and it usually happened at night. I could not find any statistics drawing a correlation between samurai who took advantage of this law drunk versus sober, but my guess is that there was usually some sake involved.

In Draconian Greece, the penalty for stealing a cabbage was death.[2] In 600 BC, most Greek laws were passed down orally, which meant that people tried to learn what was and wasn't legal via giant games of telephone. Draco was the first guy in town to inject a little consistency into the legal code. First, he decided to write down the laws so people could remember what they were. Next, he decided to simplify the penal code by making death the penalty for just about every crime (though sometimes offenders could get off easy with a lifetime of slavery). Draco's punishments were so harsh, in fact, that today the term *draconian* means overly severe or cruel.

Fun Fact: As legend would have it, Draco's death was caused by his popularity. Apparently, ancient Greek audiences showed support for a speaker by throwing their clothes at him, and one time Draco gave such a bangin' TED talk that the audience smothered him with coats and undies and he suffocated and died.[3] The universe apparently didn't take kindly to Draco having people killed for stealing cabbage. That's karma, bro.

Exporting cats was illegal in Ancient Egypt.[4] It is well known that cats were associated with gods in ancient Egypt. They were revered in both life and death. Many prominent cats were even mummified and buried with a stash (milk, food, etc.) for the afterlife. When a cat passed away, its human family members would shave off their eyebrows as a symbol of mourning.[5] What is less well known, however, is that not only were Egyptians crazy passionate about their cats, they were also super selfish with their cats. It was illegal, in fact, to export Egyptian cats to other countries, and there was an entire branch of government established to police the black market cat trade. "Ancient Egyptian Cat Cops" sounds like a really cool comic book. Too bad it would be illegal in Canada, because . . .

Prudes in the Present

Canada doesn't approve of comic books with criminal elements.[6] In 2013, the Canadian government passed Bill C-13, which was aimed at penalizing cyberbullies, revenge pornographers, and (apparently) Batman. The bill reaffirmed existing Canadian law banning the publication, sale, or distribution of "crime comics." Check this out:

> **163. (7)** In this section, "crime comic" means a magazine, periodical, or book that exclusively or substantially comprises matter depicting pictorially:
>
> (a) the commission of crimes, real or fictitious; or
> (b) events connected with the commission of crimes, real or fictitious, whether occurring before or after the commission of the crime.[7]

What is Canadian Batman supposed to do? Hunt down guys with bad attitudes? Defend Gotham from chefs with undereducated palates? How will Canadian children learn the difference between good guys and bad guys if they are never exposed to bad guys?

Luckily, there is a silver lining for C-13: It could end up helping Canadian children become more passionate lovers. In 1950, during Canada's first legislative assault on crime comics, the marketplace responded with a flood of "love comics" intended to win over the attention of teenagers.[8] Essentially they replaced "shoot-'em-ups" with "hug-it-outs," which of course resulted in Canadian baby boomers being known as the cuddliest generation (or at least that's how they should be known).*

---

* Not true.

> FAN FACT: By law, adults in Singapore must donate their organs when they die (unless they opt out of the law when they're alive).[9]
>
> —*Callum Harland, London*

Lace panties are illegal in Russia. Given the abundance of serious issues facing Russia in 2014 it came as somewhat of a shock that Russian lawmakers took time out of their busy foreign and domestic agendas to place a ban on sexy panties. How did this happen? Was it a joke? Was it a bet between Putin and his drinking buddies to see if he could inspire people to run through the streets with panties on their heads (which actually happened during protests, BTW)?

> FAN FACT: It is illegal to make a movie or TV show about time travel in China.[10]
>
> —*Joseph C., High Point, N.C.*
>
> FAN FACT: King Gustav of Sweden banned coffee in 1756. He believed it was poisonous and forced prisoners to drink it.[11]
>
> —*Vincent R., Träslövsläge, Sweden*

Iceland didn't allow ice-cold beer (or any beer) until almost thirty years ago.[12] This one blew my mind. The land of the Vikings didn't allow beer until 1989. What? Apparently, Iceland banned all alcoholic beverages about one hundred years ago. They believed drinking was unhealthy (tough to argue) and prohibition was seen as a progressive move . . . that is, until the government realized that people were going to drink anyway. Within twenty years, spirits and wine were back in legal rotation, but beer was given the cold shoulder until the Berlin Wall came down. The reason for the selective prohibition stemmed from an old Icelandic feud with Denmark. Drinking beer was seen as a largely Danish lifestyle move and the government chose to forgo frost-brewed refreshment in favor of cultural purity. Another interesting fact is that when the Icelandic government legalized alcohol they did so under the condition that all liquor stores be state owned. Drunken Monopoly, anyone?

The Ageless Innovators

Governments in Ancient Persia used to debate laws twice— once sober and once drunk—in order to make sure the idea sounded good in both states.[13] I know a lot of people who should adopt this decision-making policy on weekends. The world would be a healthier place with the following post-party logic: "I hear you, dude. Taco Bell sounds like the perfect idea right now, but we can't hit the drive-thru unless the idea also sounds good when we're sober."

In Finland, speeding ticket penalties are based on income.[14] In 2012, a Nokia executive was pulled over on his Harley for going approximately 45 mph in a 30-mph zone and was assessed a ticket that ended up costing him more than $100,000! Fines for shoplifting and some white-collar crimes are also determined by income in Finland. THIS MAKES SO MUCH SENSE that we'll never do it in North America.

In North Carolina it is illegal for a bingo game to last more than five hours (unless at a fair).[15] I'm gonna be honest, I have no idea whether this is an actual law. Having said that, the fact that it's all over the Internet warrants comment if only to point out that nobody in their right mind plays bingo for more than five hours. I don't care how much money is on the line or whether you sprinkle in side games like "Blackout" and "Texas T," bingo loses its sexy after ninety minutes, two hours tops. If this is an actual law in North Carolina, it was probably enacted to help Grandma stay lucid by making sure that she has more to focus on during the day than why "that daggum caller won't call O-66."

BONUS FACTS!

- In 1997, three men from Yemen tried to sue NASA for trespassing on Mars.[16] They claimed that they had inherited the planet from their ancestors three thousand years earlier. Unfortunately for them, they didn't win their case because there is an international treaty stating that everything in the solar system, except Earth itself, is the property of everyone on Earth.
- In China, there is an elderly rights law that makes it illegal for anyone with parents not to visit them regularly.[17]
- If police officers in Thailand misbehave they are publicly

humiliated by being forced to wear pink Hello Kitty armbands.[18]

- When the domestic parcel service was launched by the United States Postal Service in 1913, it was legal to ship children as long as they weighed less than fifty pounds.[19]
- In Churchill, Manitoba, Canada, it is illegal to lock your car in case someone needs to escape from one of the local polar bears.[20]

FAST FACTS

Questionable Judgment

- In 1919, Walt Disney was fired from his job at the *Kansas City Star* because, according to his editor, he "lacked imagination and didn't have any good ideas."[1]
- Elvis Presley failed only one class when he was in high school—music class.
- Oprah Winfrey was fired from her job as a news anchor in Baltimore because she couldn't separate her emotions from her work. Luckily, she then decided to turn her emotions into her work and proceeded to make billions.[2]
- Michael Jordan, widely considered to be the greatest basketball player ever, was left off the varsity high school basketball team in North Carolina.
- Albert Einstein's teachers told him that he was "mentally slow, unsociable, and adrift forever in his foolish dreams."

Today, Einstein is considered to be one of the smartest people ever. Good job, Teach.[3]

> FAN FACT: JFK bought twelve hundred Cuban cigars right before he signed an embargo making it illegal for anyone else to buy Cuban products.[4]
>
> —*Ignacio M., Mexico City*

- Japanese business leaders and bureaucrats tried to stymie Honda's growth in Japan because they felt that the company's founder, Soichiro Honda (and his company's culture), placed too much emphasis on individual ambition and ingenuity.[5]
- Thomas Edison's teachers in school said he was "too stupid to learn anything."[6]
- The first time Fred Astaire did a screen test for the movies, one of the studio executives wrote: "Can't act. Can't sing. Slightly bald. Can dance a little." Astaire went on to revolutionize the twentieth-century movie musical, while becoming one of the most famous dancers of all time.[7]
- Charles Schulz, the creator of Charlie Brown, Snoopy, and the rest of the Peanuts gang, had his drawings rejected by his high school yearbook.[8]
- *Harry Potter and the Sorcerer's Stone* was rejected a dozen times, and one publisher told J. K. Rowling not to quit her day job.[9]

- When Robert Heft was seventeen years old in 1958, he designed an American flag that incorporated brand-new states, Hawaii and Alaska, and submitted his work for a school project. Although his design was exactly the same as the design later adopted by the United States, Heft was awarded a B minus from his teacher.[10]

BONUS FACTS ABOUT LEADERS

- The KGB tried to blackmail former Indonesian president Achmed Sukarno with tapes of him having sex with Russian women disguised as flight attendants. Problem was, the president wasn't at all upset about being blackmailed and, in fact, he asked for more copies of the tapes to display back in his country. Hurray for the mile high club![11]
- Canadian prime minister Justin Trudeau once TKO'd a rival legislator in a charity boxing match.[12]
- Napoléon Bonaparte was buried without his penis. It was cut off during his autopsy and given to a priest in Corsica.

> FAN FACT: When a queen bee is deemed unfit to lead (due to age, disease, etc.) the worker bees cluster tightly around her body until she dies from overheating. The process is called "cuddle death."[13]
>
> —*Dylan Amos, Rockvale, Tenn.*

FAN FACT: Former Australian prime minister Bob Hawke once set a world record for "sculling" 2.5 pints of beer in eleven seconds.[14]

—*Jessica Abdallah, Melbourne, Victoria, Australia*

FAN FACT: Alexander the Great, Julius Caesar, Genghis Khan, Napoléon, Mussolini, and Hitler are all thought to have suffered from ailurophobia, the fear of cats.[15]

—*Simon Quinn, Rhode Island*

YOUTUBE CHANNEL REMIX

The Ten Greatest Prison Escapes of All Time and TripAdvisor Reviews for the Most Brutal Prisons on Earth

WE'VE ALL SEEN crazy movies about crazy jails and prison breaks, but the unbelievable capers and compounds in the movies don't seem so wild when you consider the wildest real-life prison breaks and the most extreme prisons from around the globe.

The Ten Greatest Prison Escapes of All Time

1. The Dental Floss Escape[1]

On March 17, 2000, Vincenzo Curcio escaped from prison in Turin, Italy, by sawing through the bars of his cell with dental floss. He then went old school and tied some bedsheets together, then lowered himself out a window and down to freedom.

2. Master Crafters' Escape[2]

On January 3, 1995, three inmates escaped from Britain's Parkhurst prison using tools that they built in the prison's sheet metal shop. They built a ladder long enough to scale the prison's walls, a gun (they managed to get their hands on blank ammunition), and a master key. The master key was especially impressive because the prisoners are rumored to have crafted it from memory after seeing an officer's key. For all of their ingenuity, however, the inmates neglected to consider that once they got past the prison's walls, they would still be on an island and they had no boat. . . .

3. Mother Trucker's Escape[3]

On April 11, 1998, Jay Sigler was in the courtyard of the Everglades Correctional Institution in Florida, waiting for visitors to arrive, when a Mack truck drove through the prison walls and its passengers opened fire on the prison guards. Another car followed closely behind, driven by Sigler's mother, Sandra. Sigler jumped into his mom's car and the duo took off. Unfortunately (for them) they were recaptured soon after, and in a really weird twist, Sandra Sigler would later testify against her son in order to reduce her sentence.

4. The Great Escape

Stalag Luft III was a German prisoner-of-war camp during World War II that held air force servicemen and was deemed inescapable. That was, until a few hundred prisoners hatched an elaborate escape plan together. After digging three separate tunnels, each of which was nine meters deep in order to avoid setting off the seismograph microphones along the fences, prisoners began the Great Escape on March 24, 1944. More than seventy men successfully escaped and avoided recapture. Twenty years later, the story was turned into an award-winning movie, *The Great Escape*, starring Steve McQueen.[4]

5. The Helicopter Escape[5]

In 2001, Pascal Payet had barely begun his thirty-year prison sentence when a friend of his hijacked a helicopter and broke him out of Luynes prison in France. The helicopter landed in the prison courtyard and Payet simply hopped in and flew away. However, he was recaptured two years later when he returned to the prison and attempted to break out three other inmates. In an unbelievable twist, Payet broke out once again in 2007 by boarding another hijacked helicopter in the prison courtyard. This time, when authorities recaptured him, he was locked away in a secret location that was (presumably) helicopter-proof.

> FAN FACT: In April 2006, Richard Lee McNair escaped from a prison in Louisiana by burying himself under the outgoing mail. He was recaptured a year later.[6]
> —*Michael L., Florida*

6. Texas Seven Escape[7]

On December 13, 2000, seven prisoners escaped from a maximum-security prison in Texas by overpowering and restraining nearly twenty people, including officers and inmates who weren't invited to participate. They then stole a white prison van and drove away. However, the criminals were later recaptured after they robbed a sporting goods store and killed a man in the process, which landed them on the TV show *America's Most Wanted*. They were all apprehended soon thereafter.

7. Italian Escape[8]

Antonio Ferrara, an Italian bank robber and explosives expert, escaped from prison in France when six fake police officers drove up to the prison in three fake police cruisers and opened fire on the gates with AK-47s and grenade launchers. Ferrara used a stick of dynamite (how did he get a stick of dynamite?) to blow open his cell door, ran directly into the chaos outside, and escaped in one of the cruisers. Unfortunately for him, like most everyone else on this list, he was recaptured four months later.

8. Death Camp Escape[9]

On October 14, 1943, a group of prisoners killed eleven Nazi officers inside the Sobibor prison camp and then emptied the camp's armory. Their goal was to free all six hundred prisoners in the camp; they successfully achieved half of that goal. Like the Great Escape, the escape from Sobibor was turned into a solid prison-break movie years later. In fact, the next (and last) two escapes in this chapter also made their way onto the big screen.

9. Frank Abagnale, Prison Inspector[10]

Sentenced to twelve years for multiple forgeries, Frank Abagnale Jr. was being transferred between facilities when he convinced the guards in his vehicle that he was an undercover prison inspector. The guards bought his story and soon thereafter let Abagnale walk out of the prison to meet with an "agent" (a.k.a. his criminal friend), with whom he then sped off into the night. Some of Frank Abagnale's other escapades were later chronicled on the big screen in *Catch Me If You Can*, starring Leonardo DiCaprio and Tom Hanks.

10. Escape from Alcatraz[11]

On June 11, 1962, three prisoners escaped from the island prison of Alcatraz by using dummies to convince the guards that they were asleep in their beds when in fact they were escaping through tunnels that they had dug in the prison walls *using spoons*. They then climbed through a ventilation shaft in the roof, scaled a fence, and (allegedly) crossed the frigid waters of San Francisco Bay using a raft they had constructed out of raincoats and contact cement. Nobody knows for sure if the inmates successfully crossed the bay, as they were never heard from again, nor were their bodies ever found. However, their legend lives on thanks to the 1979 movie *Escape from Alcatraz*, starring Clint Eastwood.

TripAdvisor Reviews for
the Most Brutal Prisons on Earth

Life in the free world got you down? Are you tired of visiting the same lame vacation destinations year after year? Are you ready for an immersive, all-inclusive experience? Well then, rob a bank, smack a government official, or post some libelous comments on the Internet and you could win an all-expenses-paid trip to one of the most brutal prisons on earth! Check out some of these fabulous incarceration destinations!

La Santé Prison, Paris

Location, location, location! Finally, an opportunity to visit Paris without having to interact with snooty maître d's!

La Santé is one of the most infamous prisons in France. Violence here is so pervasive that inmates are allowed out of their cells for only four hours a day.[12] Surprisingly, *La Santé Prison* translates to "prison of health." If I may, I would like to suggest a rebranding. The prison should adopt a name more representative of the lifestyle, such as "horrific dimly lit prison of death," or something. I feel like that would be a nice juxtaposition for the City of Light.

> FAN FACT: In 1386, a pig in France was convicted of murder and executed by public hanging.[13]
>
> —*Ethan Martin Cynthiana, Kentucky*

Petak Island Prison, Russia[14]

A secluded boutique retreat in the heart of fabulous Siberia!

This maximum-security prison is home to Russia's worst criminals. It's located on an island in White Lake, one of the ten largest lakes in Europe, and prisoners are only allowed two visitors per year. Because of complete isolation, lack of basic facilities, and bitter cold, most residents of the prison go insane well before their sentences are completed. Come to think of it, isolation and freezing cold temperatures sounds like the life of a Canadian YouTuber. And you all wonder why I'm so weird.

Cotonou Civil Prison, Benin, Africa[15]

Escape the rat race (but not the rats) and settle into the laid-back pace of Benin!

This prison holds twenty-four hundred men, women, and children in an institution built to hold four hundred. Disturbingly, over 90 percent of inmates here are awaiting trial for alleged crimes because of a backlog in the country's judicial system and lack of funds from the Republic. It can take several years just to be seen by a jury. Cells are so overcrowded that prisoners have to sleep in shifts!

Camp 22, North Korea[16]

Get off the grid in North Korea!

Gaining international attention in 2012 after its warden defected to China, Camp 22 is an isolated prison for political prisoners. Able to hold up to fifty thousand prisoners, it is a large compound that (allegedly) has held entire families and sometimes even generations of offspring. Prisoners are subject to torture and even human experimentation, where they become lab rats for biological weapons such as anthrax, and suffer other brutalities including bomb testing. Satellite imagery is inconclusive as to whether the camp is still open today, but the legacy lives on in nightmares all over the world.

THE CULTURE CLUBS

Ten Extreme Initiations from Around the World

IT'S AMAZING WHAT people will do in order to be accepted by their peers. As a college student in Canada, I thought waiting in line for an hour outside a nightclub in the freezing snow was "extreme." However, compared to what other people around the world go through to get into their "clubs," I got off easy. Super easy.

The Bullet Ant Gloves of the Sateré-Mawé[1] Deep in Brazil there is a type of ant known as the "bullet ant," which earned its name because its sting hurts like a gunshot. In order to be considered a man in the Sateré-Mawé tribe, boys must wear gloves that are filled with bullet ants and, get this—it's not just a onetime ritual. Boys must wear the gloves *twenty times* in order to prove that they are worthy of the responsibilities of adulthood. Did I mention that bites from bullet ants hurt thirty times worse than bee stings? Also, the boys wear the gloves for ten minutes at a time and the stinging and burning *gets worse* after the gloves come off as waves of pain often roll through the affected areas for up to twenty-four hours.[2] Jeez. All I had to do to become a man was turn eighteen and survive my first hangover.

Hells Angels "Urine-itiation"[3] The most famous motor-cycle gang on the planet is known for being ruthless, loyal, and tough as nails. Apparently, it is also pretty stinky because in order to be initiated into the gang, candidates must lie on the ground as existing members dump human poop and pee on their jeans and jackets. Worse, the newbies aren't allowed to wash their clothes afterward. This confuses me on a number of levels. I get the idea of wanting pledges to go through hell and back in order to prove their worth, but if the new members smell like outhouses, then life is nasty for the old members who have to hang out with them. Who wants to ride around town with a human outhouse? Reason No. 487 why I'm not in a biker gang.

Hamar Cattle Jumping[4] The Hamar tribe of Ethiopia are cattle herders, which is why it makes sense for them to use cows in their manhood ritual. Having said that, their bull-running ceremony is pretty crazy. You thought North American cowboys had guts? Well, eight seconds on one animal doesn't sound so hard when compared to one second on twenty-five animals. Let me explain. In order to become a man, boys must run across the backs of ten to thirty lined-up cattle without falling. Did I mention the boys run naked? And that they have to make it across the line four times? Did I mention that the cattle have all been castrated, which one would think might make them a bit irritable?

Native American Vision Quest[5] Of all the rituals on this list, the vision quest stands out as the most appealing rite of passage to me. In fact, even though I am neither Native American nor a boy (debatable), the idea of spending a few days alone in the wilderness listening to nature and my body and opening myself up to dreams sounds wonderful. Sure, I would get hungry and all the bumps in the night would terrify me as I slept without a tent on the bare ground, but that's kind of what being a grown-up is, right? Facing up to fears, overcoming obstacles, and trying to focus on what is really important in your life. If I didn't have to make several YouTube videos this week, I would go right now.

Aboriginal Walkabout[6] The vision quest is merely a warm-up in comparison with the Australian aboriginal walkabout, in which twelve- or thirteen-year-old boys go off into the wilderness for up to six months in order to connect with nature and spirituality, and to learn about themselves. They use the ancient songs of their ancestors as "song lines" to help guide their journey. Again, I can't help but envision how I would have fared on my own at thirteen years old, and I'll tell you what, the answer isn't good. The closest I ever got to a walkabout was spending a weekend scanning the woods for secret passages in *The Legend of Zelda*.

Bohemian Club Waiting List[7] Former presidents, rock stars, industry barons, and famous intellectuals are all said to have been members of Northern California's supersecretive and selective Bohemian Club. There are several weird rituals that are rumored to take place on the club's annual retreat in the redwood forest, but in this case I'm more interested in the club's waiting list than the sacrifices, flaming effigies, and other initiation rituals conducted by the frat boys Masters circuit. Depending on what you read, the waiting list for Bohemian Club is somewhere between fifteen and thirty years long! Let me say straight out that I don't buy this statistic for a second. Fame and power are both fleeting, and organizations that pride themselves on exclusivity and status need to bring in members at their societal peak. Wait twenty years for a rock star and you're likely to induct a broken-down has-been (probably trying to reinvent himself as a country artist) into your club. The mind-blowing initiation ritual here would be for someone to actually wait his turn on the list.

Drinking Blood with Turkish Freemasons[8] The Freemasons began in the fourteenth century as a fraternal industry association for stonemasons, and in the six hundred–plus years since then has existed as the world's archetype for sinister societies. Every now and again crazy details about the Masons and their rituals will be revealed in an exposé, and in 1997 a Turkish hidden camera did just that. In a video about the Masons that ended up running on Turkish television, men are seen performing satanic rituals and one guy even drinks the blood of a goat. Apparently only the thirty-third-degree masons are allowed to drink goat blood. What I want to know is what special privileges are awarded for achieving higher degrees of status. What are fifth-degree Masons, a title known as Perfect Master, allowed to do? Also, how is it possible to have twenty-eight titles that rank higher than Perfect Master? So many questions . . .

Algonquin Indian Trip[9] The goal of this manhood ritual is to clear a young man of his childhood so that he can look forward to manhood. That said, the ritual is so intense that the Algonquins of Quebec don't let boys do it until they are twenty-one years old. Aspiring adults spend twenty-one days in a cage, tripping on a crazy hallucinogen called datura. The purpose of the drug is to wipe out childhood memories, *Men in Black*–style (one of the side effects of datura is memory loss). Thing is, datura has lots of other side effects, including loss of speech and movement, elevated heart rate, violent behavior, hallucinations, and, of course, death. Once the hallucinations stop, the boy stays in the cage until the side effects wear off. Good luck! My guess is that the ritual also teaches young men to say no to drugs in the future.

The Nigerian Iria Ceremony[10] Hey, ladies! Don't want you to think I forgot about you. Women have extreme rites of passage, too. In some native Nigerian tribes, girls go through the Iria ritual to help prepare them for womanhood. While the details of the Iria vary depending on community and tribe, the consistent stages of the ritual seem to be successive phases of stripping down and fattening up. First, a young woman strips naked in the center of her community in order to bare it all in front of her peers and elders. Next she goes to fattening tents, where she spends weeks eating nonstop and avoiding movement, except for bathing. Finally, she returns from the fattening tents and is celebrated by her family and friends. Basically, this ritual is the exact opposite of what happens on the American television show *The Biggest Loser*.

Land Diving in Vanuatu[11] X Games athletes can't hold a candle to the land-diving men on the island of Pentecost, Vanuatu. Land diving is basically bungee jumping's crazy great-grandfather. The men erect towers out of sticks and vines that can reach a hundred feet high and then they jump off the structures with nothing to break their falls except the vines tied to their ankles. Their goal is to get as close to the ground as possible without smashing into it. Talk about a test of courage (and sanity)! Over the years, land divers have gotten more scientific in their approach, measuring the vines to fit the height and weight of each diver. However, that is not to say that there aren't a few miscalculations here and there. For example, consider the following anecdote from ABCNews.com:

> When Britain's Queen Elizabeth visited Vanuatu in 1974, the Pentecost islanders put on a land diving show for her. However, it was the wrong season and the vines were dry—so they snapped, with diver after diver hitting the ground. One of them later died, the only fatality in living memory.

Whoops! The most amazing part of this story is the fragment "*with diver after diver hitting the ground.*" Why wouldn't they reassess their measurements after the first guy kissed the turf? I'm pretty sure that I would rather complete every other crazy initiation on this list than prove my manhood as a land diver.

> FAN FACT: The aardvark is the only member of a club called *Tubulidentata*, meaning "tube teeth."[12]
>
> —*Angie F., Pittsburgh, Pa.*

SPECIAL SECTION:
THE NAME GAME

Fame Name

SIDEBURNS WERE NAMED after an American Civil War general named Ambrose Burnside, who was known for his unusual facial hair.[1] Maybe the good general knew what the rest of society would learn a century later: Growing facial hair can have health benefits, such as protecting you from the sun, preventing asthma attacks, and even slowing the aging process.

- One of the developers of the modern toilet was Thomas Crapper; hence the origin of the phrase "take a crap."[2]

- The department store JCPenney is named for its founder, James Cash Penney.[3] I can't understand why he used an abbreviation. His middle name was Cash and he was opening a retail store. What could be better than that? As an aside, Cash Penney would be an amazing name for a rapper.
- The margarita cocktail was purportedly named after Margaret "Margarita" Sames, a woman from Texas who concocted the beverage as a refreshing poolside drink. Good thing her nickname wasn't Gertrude.[4]
- The term *maverick* is based on a wealthy Texas landlord named Samuel Maverick. Maverick didn't want to hurt his cows by branding them with a hot iron, so he left their hides unmarked. His cows were easily recognizable, therefore, because they were the only herd that didn't bear the name of an owner.[5]

> FAN FACT: Akon, the famous rapper, has a very long Senagalese name: Aliaume Damala Badara Akon Thiam. Akon is actually just one of his (several) middle names.[6]
>
> —*Rajveer Dhakan, Dubai, United Arab Emirates*

Same Name

- Edward Jones[7] is a Missouri-based investment firm with more than ten thousand locations scattered across the United States. The firm was founded in 1922 by an investor named Edward D. Jones. Amazingly, forty years earlier, a different Edward D. Jones was a cofounder of Dow Jones & Company. He and his partner, Charles Dow, are the namesakes of the Dow Jones Industrial Average stock market index. *However*, forty years before that another Edward Jones was making a name for himself as a famous Buckingham Palace intruder. Boy Jones, as the press called him, famously broke into the palace as a teenager and stole the Queen's underwear!

- Anne Hathaway is the Academy Award–winning movie star of such films as *Les Misérables*, *The Devil Wears Prada*, and *Rio*. Despite her success, however, the actress isn't nearly the most famous owner of her name. That distinction goes to Shakespeare's wife, Anne Hathaway,[8] who also happens to be one of history's most famous cougars. When Hathaway married Shakespeare, she was twenty-six years old and he was only eighteen!

- In 2015, Walter J. Palmer,[9] a dentist from Minnesota, became public enemy No. 1 on the Internet after he went to Africa and (potentially illegally) shot and killed a beloved lion named Cecil. When pictures of the kill surfaced on social media, the world collectively freaked out, but one man took the news worse than most—the one other Walter J. Palmer in the local phone book. The moment the scandal hit, the eighty-year-old former insurance salesman started receiving harassing phone calls and abusive threats from complete strangers.

- Edgar Allan Poe's 1838 novella *The Narrative of Arthur Gordon Pym of Nantucket* features a sailor named Richard Parker who gets eaten by his crewmates after their boat is set adrift at sea (he drew the short straw in their hunger game). Less than fifty years later, after a huge storm destroyed an English vessel off the coast of Australia, the ship's four-man crew decided to stave off starvation by eating the cabin boy, whose name was (wait for it) Richard Parker.[10]

- Five years after John Lennon's assassination in 1980, production started on a made-for-TV movie about the Beatles singer and his lady, Yoko Ono, titled *John and Yoko*. An up-and-coming actor named Mark Chapman was initially hired to play the lead role, even though Mark Chapman was also the name of the man who had assassinated John Lennon. Once executives realized the unfortunate coincidence, they cut Chapman (the actor) loose and recast the role.[11]

Shame in a Name

Some people have names so horrible that they really have no choice but to turn to a life of crime. Here are a couple of examples:

- In 2010, Canadian law enforcement arrested an American fugitive who was wanted for several creepy crimes involving children and pornography. The pervert's name: Patrick Molesti.[12]

- Crystal Metheny never had a chance. The Florida woman was once arrested for firing a "missile" into a car and has also accumulated multiple drug charges.[13] What did her parents think was going to happen with a name like Crystal Metheny?

Overcame the Name

Luckily a bad name doesn't guarantee a life of crime and failure. In fact, several athletes have (I suspect) used their awkward names as motivation to prove the world wrong and achieve greatness in sports.

- Wang Liqin was a dominant Chinese table tennis player in the mid-2000s.[14]
- Ivana Mandic earned a college basketball scholarship at the University of Charlotte.[15]
- Destinee Hooker knew that her destiny was to shrug off her awkward name and become a member of the United States women's volleyball team.
- Minnesota was a hotbed for athletes with awkward names in the 1970s.[16] Rusty Kuntz played for the Minnesota Twins baseball team, while Dick Paradise played hockey for the Minnesota Fighting Saints.

Reclaim the Name

In 2011, city officials in Fort Wayne, Indiana, couldn't decide on a name for their new county building. They knew they wanted to name it after a famous Fort Wayne citizen but they couldn't reach a consensus, so they decided to ask the people of Fort Wayne to vote online for the name of their choice. Unlike the government officials, the citizens of Fort Wayne quickly united behind a single candidate, long-serving Fort Wayne former mayor Harry Baals. Unfortunately, some of the city leaders weren't comfortable with the idea of their new "jewel" being called the Harry Baals Government Center; they decided to call the building Citizens Square.[17]

Part 2

WHO CAME UP WITH THAT?

THE WACKIEST
MASCOTS ON EARTH

THE FRENCH OPERA *La Mascotte* tells the story of a down-on-his-luck farmer who brings a beautiful girl, Bettina, to his farm for good luck. He, along with the rest of the guys in the neighborhood, believes that Bettina will bring good fortune to whatever house she stays in, so long as she remains a virgin. Naturally, a fierce competition for her ... uh ... "luck" ensues.[1] When the opera premiered in 1880, it was an instant sensation. The following year it premiered in both the United States and England and in doing so introduced the English-speaking world to the concept of the modern mascot. Quickly, businesses, sports teams, churches, and schools began to adopt their own lucky characters. Fast-forward almost 140 years and it seems every business and every family has its own animal, vegetable, or mineral mascot, which means that choosing the ten wackiest is a nearly impossible task. But "nearly impossible" will never be enough to dissuade a Canadian explorer like me. And I'll tell you what, it's hard to argue with the creepy creatures on this list.

Wackiest Health Ambassador:
Senhor Testiculo, the Brazilian Testicular Cancer Mascot[2]
A few years back, the brain trust from the Associação de Assistência às Pessoas com Câncer (Association for the Assistance of People with Cancer) in the Brazilian city of Viçosa thought, "What better way to get men to check themselves for testicular cancer than by threatening to haunt their dreams with a disturbing mascot that they will never be able to unsee?" Soon thereafter, Senhor Testiculo was born. Senhor Testiculo is, for lack of a better term, a big happy nut sack with goofy eyes and randomly distributed curly hairs all over his face/balls. If that image isn't disturbing enough on its own, Mr. Testicles also wears a disturbingly vacant grin and he only has two teeth, one on the top and one on the bottom. Naturally, he's a hit at family-friendly events in his Brazilian community.

Can you imagine being the guy who wears the Senhor Testiculo costume? What happens when your girlfriend brings you home to meet her parents?

"So, Paulo, what do you do for work?"

"Uh . . . I work in health care."

"Are you a doctor?"

"Not exactly."

"A nurse?"

"No. Actually, I dress up as a creepy nut sack and hug children at festivals."

"If you ever contact my daughter again I will cut off your testiculos."

Wackiest Olympic Mascot: Misha the (Serial Killer) Bear— Russian Olympic Mascot 1980

The Olympics have a rich and storied history of parading creepy mascots into the stadium to fire up fans and terrorize children. Choosing the weirdest Olympic mascot of all time is like choosing the most mind-blowing Olympic performance of all time because there are so many amazing options to choose from. For example, Schneemann (snowman), the 1976 Innsbruck Winter Olympics mascot, had the creepy large hands, feet, and eyes of a classic cartoon monster.[3] The Nagano Winter Olympics in 1998 featured the Snowlets,[4] four owls that appear to be ancestors of the Angry Birds, as drawn by a five-year-old. Wikipedia describes Neve and Gliz,[5] the mascots of the 2006 Turin Winter Olympics, as humanized versions of a snowball and an ice cube, which would be weird enough on its own to take the crown . . . but then there's Misha.

On the surface, Misha, the bear cub that represented the 1980 Moscow Summer Olympics, appears to be one of the more conservative mascot choices. However, while Misha's body is cute and cuddly, his eyes are open *way* too wide, freezing his face into the same maniacal expression that Jack Nicholson had in *The Shining*. Given Stephen King's fascination with writing about animal killers in the '80s, it's astonishing to me that he never based a novel on Misha, the Russian serial killer bear cub.[6]

The worst part about being the guy who wore the Misha costume is that in communist USSR, the job was likely assigned to him. Then again, for all we know Misha could have been an undercover Soviet spy who was sent to the Olympics to obtain confidential information from Western world leaders.

Wackiest College Mascot: The Wichita State Shocker

Ever since the Wichita State University men's basketball team made a Cinderella run during the 2013 NCAA tournament, all of North America has developed an obsession with their mascot, the Shocker, a.k.a. WuShock. Is it a tampon? Is it a firework? Is its haircut intentionally styled to be the perfect hybrid of Lloyd's and Harry's coifs from the *Dumb and Dumber* movies? Add in the freaky and slightly disturbing sexual connotation of the term *shocker* and you have an ironclad résumé for the list of weird worldly mascots. In 2014, the *New York Times* shared a slide show of WuShock's evolution, beginning in the 1950s when a cheerleader built the first costume with his mom (sigh for that guy). The slide show then chronicled every iteration through the steroid-enhanced present-day version.[7] The slides are worth a look because every version of the wheat beast is creepy in its unique way.

Wackiest Municipal Mascot: Manbe-Kun—Oshamanbe, Japan

With the body of a lobster, the face of a gingerbread man on acid, and the Twitter feed recklessness of Donald Trump,

Manbe-Kun, the official mascot for the town of Oshamanbe, Japan, was a shoo-in for this list. In August 2011, Manbe-Kun stirred up controversy by tweeting a series of incendiary messages in conjunction with the anniversary of the end of World War II, talking about the three million Japanese people who died during the war and the twenty million Asian casualties. WTF, Manbe-Kun? One has to wonder if writing about local fish festivals and school graduations finally got to the lobster-bread man. Little Manbe clearly snapped (and that is not a reference to his claws). "No matter how you look at it," he tweeted, "Japan's war of aggression started everything."[8] Needless to say, Manbe-Kun's sharp tongue brought shame upon his municipal government, not to mention his species (assuming there are others).

Wackiest Human Mascot: Chacha Cricket (Uncle Cricket)— Pakistani National Cricket Team

The only actual human on this list, Chacha Cricket (whose real name is Chaudhry Abdul Jalil),[9] is such a Pakistani cricket superfan that the Pakistan Cricket Board (PCB) has sponsored his travel to ensure that he is present wherever the national team plays. With his free-flowing white beard and similarly free-flowing green outfit, the only cricket mascot more popular than Jiminy looks a bit like an Amish Gandalf.

Wackiest Soccer Mascot: Kingsley—Scottish Football (Soccer) Mascot

Up until 2015, the Partick Thistle Football Club in Scotland was represented by Jaggy MacBee, a mascot that appeared to be the less talented, less photogenic cousin of the bee on the Honey Nut Cheerios box. However, that all changed when award-winning British artist David Shrigley designed Mac-Bee's inexplicable replacement, Kingsley the Sun. Upon seeing the unibrow-sporting, mouth-breathing catastrophe of a mascot for the first time, the British press went berserk. "It looks like Lisa Simpson after years of mind-bending drugs," wrote one journalist.[10] "Opposition will be intimidated," responded Shrigley, "and we will be able to triumph over them." Personally, I think Kingsley looks like he should be on a bottle of generic SunnyD.

Wackiest World Cup Mascot: Ciao—1990 Italy
World Cup Mascot

Not to be outdone by the Olympics, the World Cup has consistently trotted out some pretty strange mascots every four years. Juanito, the Mexican mascot of 1970, looked a little too young and too chubby for the pitch. Naranjito, the soccer-playing orange from Spain, was 1982's version of the Annoying Orange. And Footix, the 1998 World Cup rooster from France, appears to be wearing a Snuggie.[11] But all of these creatures pale in comparison to Ciao, the Italian mascot of the 1990 World Cup.[12] Ciao looks like an unraveled Rubik's Cube or a Jenga tower in the midst of falling over. Not only that, but Ciao is positioned to deliver a devastating knee to a soccer ball, which would be fine except for the fact that *his head is also a soccer ball.*

Wackiest Live Animal Mascot:
Wojtek, the Polish Soldier Bear[13]

The more I read about the lone live-animal mascot on this list, the more his story blows my mind. In 1942, a group of Polish soldiers were walking through Iran when they came upon a small boy with a large bundle, a malnourished bear cub whose mother had been shot. The soldiers took the bear with them and raised him as World War II was going on, which on its own would be cool enough for inclusion in this list; however, when you add in that Wojtek wrestled with the soldiers, drank beer from a bottle, ate cigarettes (it was a different time, people), and *ran supplies back and forth during battle*, this bear might be the captain of the mind-blowing mascot team. *But*—the coolest story about the soldier bear is that apparently he even

caught a thief who broke into the ammunition compound where Wojtek was sleeping. Can you imagine being that thief? He surely considered a lot of different variables before sneaking into the Polish ammunition compound, but no way would he have envisioned having to deal with a beer-drinking bear security guard. These tales of heroism (and others) are the reason that during the war, Wojtek earned official military rank from the Polish army, and why he was seen as a national hero until his death in 1963.

Wackiest Retail Mascot: Open Chan— Taiwanese 7-Eleven Mascot

According to 7-Eleven's Taiwan website,[14] Open Chan, "a dog who comes from the Open planet," is "the first cartoon spokesperson in the convenience retailing industry of Taiwan." I've never been to the Open planet, but on my planet, dogs don't wear rainbow-shaped helmets and they don't look like zombie versions of the Pillsbury Doughboy. But what do I know? Open Chan was popular enough in Taiwan that, in addition to pushing slushies, he/she also released an album, *Open Chan Music Party*, complete with the following four songs: "Open Your Dream," "Lock Your Luck,"[15] "Together Forever," and "Love Song." "Lock Your Luck" is particularly catchy and reminds me of early Avril Lavigne (along with every Disney Channel sitcom theme song ever made).

Wackiest Corporate Mascot: Fukuppy—Japanese Manufacturing Mascot

Sometimes the name says it all. In 2013, Fukushima Industries was hurting from a brand standpoint because consumers were mistakenly associating their brand with the location of Japan's massive nuclear meltdown two years earlier (the two are unrelated). Unfortunately, unveiling their new mascot only fanned the guilt-by-association flames. The look of their new mascot, a smiling egg with shoes and wings, was pretty weird on its own, but not weird enough (by Japanese standards) to set the Internet ablaze. In this case, Fukushima's attempt to get cute with the egg's name is what got them in trouble. What they wanted to do was combine their company name, Fukushima, with the English word *happy*, so they simply pressed the two words together and made *Fukuppy*. That's right, folks. The company trotted out a crackable mascot with a name seemingly derived from the phrase "fuck up." Throw in the association with the country's biggest nuclear "fukuppy" of the century and you've got the makings of an unintentionally hilarious mascot mistake. Needless to say, the company quickly issued an apology and promised to "look into the name, including a rethink of it."[16] Good rethink, guys. Good rethink.

CREATIVE COURTSHIPS FROM ACROSS THE GLOBE

(And America's Most Common Love Story)

GIVEN THE RIDICULOUS speed and convenience of modern-day dating, it would be hypocritical to suggest that the courtship rituals of previous eras and/or distant cultures are more "extreme" than swiping right for love. I predict that one day soon there could very well be a virtual reality dating app that allows singles to go on first dates as holograms. In comparison to holograms, in-laws hiring private detectives in India seems downright tame. That said, presenting the object of your affection with a severed head or giving your main squeeze an apple slice from your armpit (both real and in this chapter) probably still qualifies as extreme. However, as a gesture of cultural awareness and tolerance, I will simply refer to the courtship rituals on this list as "creative."

Leasing Love in Thailand[1]

In many cultures throughout the world, it is common for money to exchange hands when a man and woman get married. In some cultures, the bride brings a dowry of money, land, livestock, etc., to her husband, while in other places the husband pays the family of his bride-to-be for the right to marry her. Regardless of who pays whom, the deals are almost always binding, permanent symbols of commitment . . . except in some areas of Thailand, where apparently it's cool to lease your lover. In these places, money changes hands, but if the man or woman isn't satisfied with the merchandise, there is a negotiated period in which he or she can return the goods. Although these leases on love might seem a little crazy at first, when compared to the "all sales are final" policies of most arranged marriages, the short-term-rental market seems pretty logical. After all, that's what we do in the Western world, isn't it? We spend lots of money and time dating other people without a full-time commitment. Our model is much more of a rent-to-own marriage marketplace, even though that isn't the most romantic way to think about love. Maybe the term *layaway* is better . . . or maybe not.

Marriage Fairs in China[2]

China has turned into the world's biggest sausage fest. Here's the problem: The country used to have a strict one-child-per-household policy that resulted in families "trying harder" (euphemism of the century) to have boys than girls, which led to a birth ratio of 120 boys to 100 girls, according to Forbes. That 20 percent bonus in the "boys" column translates to a surplus of tens of millions of dudes. If dating is a large game of musical chairs, that means millions of young Chinese men will be left without a seat when the music stops. On the flip side, the dramatic imbalance means that women and their families have a lot more leverage when selecting potential husbands. In fact, marriage markets have sprung up all over China, which operate like career fairs, except instead of dropping off your résumé and head shots for potential employers, you discuss job history with potential in-laws.

"Hmmm. Your résumé says you are six feet five but you look to be more like five feet six. You're not trying to pull a Stallone on me, are you? Because I don't have time for short grandchildren."

> FAN FACT: The longest kiss ever lasted for fifty-eight hours and thirty-five minutes and took place in Thailand in 2013.[3]   —*Alexander L., Scotland*

The Private Dick Market in India[4]

Premarital due diligence has long been a part of Indian culture. Before big cities were built, the responsibility of digging up personal dirt on potential brides and grooms fell to, according to the *Los Angeles Times*, "the village priests, matchmakers, and busybodies" (was "village busybody" a full-time job?). Since urbanization, Indian snooping has been handed off to private dicks (detectives), who keep their watchful eyes out for men and women with fudged histories and résumés who are trying to jump up a caste or two in society. The majority of marriages in India are still arranged, and parents want to make sure that they have picked a suitable match for their sons and daughters. During the investigations, the detectives will not only stake out houses and tail their targets to social spots and work, but the dicks will also role-play as partygoers in order to test commitment. Some detectives even pose as market researchers and offer their targets free merchandise in exchange for answering some personal questions. "Hey, want a free generic iPhone? All you have to do is answer questions about your relationship. Don't worry, your answers will only be shared with our company . . . and all of your future in-laws, who will use these answers against you for the rest of your life."

Kickapoo Whistling in Mexico[5]

This is just plain cool. For generations, young Kickapoo guys and gals have been whistling sweet nothings back and forth to their squeezes in code. Here's how it works. Basically, one or more guys will post up at a central meeting spot after dark, at which point they will start whistling loudly to their ladies. However, this isn't a construction worker's catcall we're talking about here. Although the guys are whistling loudly and in public, their messages are intended only for the ears of their ladies, with whom they will have essentially designed their own special courtship code based on tone, cadence, melody, etc. When a girl steps out of her house to answer back (via whistle) to tell her guy that she'll be there in a second, or that her parents have her on lockdown, or just that she's thinking of him, everybody in the village will know that she's hookin' up, but nobody will know who she's hookin' up with. Pretty awesome. The one downside is that Kickapoo whistling sort of destroys the idea of casual dating because every time you want to flirt with a girl you have to make up a whole new whistle-code language. Also, I wonder how many Kickapoo guys end up having to sleep on the sofa after accidentally whistling their ex-girlfriends' code.

Severed Heads in Taiwan[6]

Up until the early twentieth century, the men of the Atayal tribe in Taiwan had a unique and very bold approach to wooing the ladies. Instead of giving his lady candy or flowers or sending thoughtful handwritten notes, a man would present the apple of his eye with the severed head of a slain enemy. Apparently the macho (and, I have to assume, messy) gesture showed the women of the tribe that the guys were mature and successful providers. I can't believe that Hollywood hasn't made a time machine movie in which an Atayal warrior is brought to present day, falls in love in the suburbs of Cleveland, and presents his lady with the severed head of the douchey captain of the football team. How would she respond if she knew he was from the past? You'd buy a ticket to that movie, right? Let the record show I thought of this idea first!

Armpit Apple[8]

What's the best gift to give the apple of your eye? How about an apple from your armpit? Imagine this, ladies: You and your girls get all dressed up and go out to the club. The guys are watching you and you are watching them. The bass is thumping and everybody is sweating and bouncing and having a ball. At some point in the evening, you notice a particular guy who stands out from the crowd. How do you let him know you're interested without being weird about it? Well, if you lived in Austria back in the day, you would give him an apple slice. And not just any slice, mind you, but the slice you've been hiding in your armpit all night. Sound crazy? Of course it does! But that's what used to happen at fancy balls (hee hee) in Vienna. Women would present their underarm fruit to their prospective Prince Charmings and if the guys felt the same way about the gal, they would *eat the sweaty apple*. Here's my biggest non-hygiene-related issue with this: What do you (the lady) do after a guy bites your apple? You certainly don't want to go home with that guy, right? I mean he just inhaled some five-hour armpit. Something tells me this custom began as a practical joke.

Get Pussy (Willow) Whipped on Dyngus Day[9]

Dyngus Day is a Polish party that takes place close to Easter and celebrates Polish culture and courtship. How do you let a lady know you're feelin' her vibe on Dyngus Day? Simple: You gently whip her with a switch from the pussy willow tree and then hope that she responds by drenching you with water or by throwing a different object at your head. Sounds a lot like kindergarten flirting to me. In fact, had someone told me in kindergarten that there was a holiday called Dyngus Day, it would have immediately jumped onto the podium with Christmas and Halloween.

> FAN FACT: Napoléon Bonaparte wrote a romance novella titled *Clisson and Eugénie*.[10]
> —*Anthony Steele Mandan, North Dakota*

Get Your Government-Issued Freak On in Singapore[11]

In the early 1980s the government of Singapore noticed that its wealthy and well-educated citizens weren't getting married and having babies at a high enough rate to sustain the population, so it decided to step in and help the fancy people get freaky. The government formed the Social Development Unit (SDU) to address the problem. The SDU offered activities ranging from dance lessons to personal coaching to singles cruises. That's right, a government-sponsored love boat to the Maldives, all in hopes of getting people to hook up and settle down. In 2009, the SDU was rebranded as the SDN (Social Development Network) and has since added several new features, including personal ads and online chat functions, while also partnering with dating companies from the private sector. This one really takes the expression "Big Brother is watching" to the next level. More like "Big Brother is my wingman." Pretty creepy, if you ask me. What are successful matches supposed to tell their children? "Your mother and I fell in love with the assistance of a state-sponsored program aimed at creating you. Any other questions, Little Terminator?"

> FAN FACT: In order to determine the right time to mate, a male giraffe will continuously head-butt the female in the bladder until she urinates. The male then tastes the pee and determines whether or not the female is ovulating.[12]
>
> —*Zayd Bawab, Toronto, Ontario, Canada*

Moving In in Ancient Egypt[13]

In sharp contrast to the voyeuristic modern-day government of Singapore, the ancient Egyptians believed that marriage was a private arrangement and the government took no interest in it or even kept records of it. Instead of a legally binding agreement, marriage was simply an arrangement made between two people and their families that the man and woman would shack up and eventually start a family. Sounds like there were some hippies in ancient Egypt.

"Hey man, is it cool if your son and I shack up and maybe spend the rest of our lives together, or whatever? All right, righteous. We'll have you over for some roasted goat and we can all worship the cat."

The Most Popular Love Story in America

Michael and Ashley met through friends[*] (with whom they have since lost touch[†]) and were immediately attracted to each other. Michael[‡] was twenty-six years old and Ashley[§] was twenty-four. Little did they know they would be married 2.8 years[¶] after their first date at Starbucks.[**] Michael picked Ashley up in his Ford Focus[††] and in order to make her feel comfortable, he played recognizable songs like the Spice Girls' "Wannabe" and Lou Bega's "Mambo No. 5."[‡‡] Although Michael had no way of knowing it, Ashley decided she wanted a second

[*] Thirty percent of married couples are introduced through friends. http://www.wsj.com/articles/SB10001424052702303325204579463272000371990

[†] Falling in love comes at the cost of losing two close friends. http://www.bbc.com/news/science-environment-11321282

[‡] Michael was the most popular male baby name of 1990.

[§] Ashley was the most popular female baby name of 1992.

[¶] On average, couples get married 2.8 years after showing romantic interest. The average age of a man getting married for the first time is twenty-nine; it's twenty-seven for women. http://www.eharmony.com/blog/when-dating-how-long-do-you-wait-for-the-ring/#.VZGfEu1Viko

[**] Starbucks is the most popular first-date spot in America. http://mashable.com/2015/04/09/first-date-popular-spots/

[††] The Ford Focus is the most popular car in the world, driven primarily by its demand overseas. http://www.forbes.com/sites/joannmuller/2013/12/23/the-worlds-most-popular-cars-ford-focus-and-other-surprises/

[‡‡] "Wannabe" and "Mambo No. 5" are the two most recognizable songs of all time. http://ceoworld.biz/2014/11/04/top-20-recognizable-songs-time. Michael stopped short of playing the third most recognizable song, "Eye of the Tiger," because he didn't want to add undue pressure to the date, or risk turning the experience into a montage.

date with him before they even reached the coffee shop;* she knew she wanted to be exclusive with him pretty soon thereafter, although they didn't title their relationship until their seventh date. Seven dates after that they traded apartment keys, said, "I love you," and the rest is history.†

BONUS FACTS!

- Other people see you as 20 percent more attractive than you think you are. When you look in the mirror all you see are your looks, not your personality.[14]
- Falling in love produces a high similar to that of cocaine.[15]

---

* Forty percent of people worldwide decide whether they want to have a second date within two to three minutes of a first date. http://www.timeout.com/dating-2015/
† Most couples get into exclusive relationships after six to eight dates, and they swap apartment keys between the twelfth and fourteenth dates. http://thoughtcatalog .com/nico-lang/2013/08/29-eye-opening-dating-facts-that-will-change-the-way -you-view-relationships/

FAST FACTS

Invention Reinvention

- The modern-day Kevlar bulletproof vest was developed by a pizza delivery guy named Richard Davis, after he was shot twice while making deliveries.
- Bubble wrap was originally invented in 1957 to be sold as wallpaper.[1]
- The small pocket inside the large pocket of your jeans was originally designed for pocket watches.[2]
- Spanx was invented by a fax machine saleswoman, Sara Blakely, who cut the feet off her control-top pantyhose and wore them under her outfits for comfort and to make her legs look slimmer.[3]
- The modern handshake dates all the way back to the fifth century BC, when swordsmen would greet each other with their weapon hand free in order to show that they came in peace.[4]

- Viagra was initially invented as a treatment for hypertension and heart disease.[5]
- According to legend, potato chips were developed by George Crum, a restaurateur with an annoying customer who kept sending his french fries back to the kitchen, claiming they were too soggy. Crum wanted to shut the guy up so he sliced the potatoes extra thin, fried them over and over, and covered them in salt. Welcome to the world, potato chip.[6]

> **FAN FACT:** No one knows who invented the fire hydrant because the patent burned in a fire. Ironic much?[7]
> —*Hibiki Kagami, Fairfax, Va.*
>
> **FAN FACT:** The person who designed the modern Frisbee was cremated after he died, and his ashes were molded into Frisbees.[8]
> —*Lenin I., Orlando, Fla.*

YOUTUBE CHANNEL REMIX

Amazing Creatures Created by Science and the Craziest Drugs You Never Knew Existed

IT IS HARD to top Mother Nature's designs, but that hasn't stopped mad scientists all over the globe from trying to pimp both her critters and her chemical compounds. Whether the modifications were made to enhance food, mood, or pets, the crazy concoctions in this chapter are intense, mind-boggling, and, in some cases, dangerous and horrifying.

Amazing Creatures Created by Science

Glow-in-the-Dark Pets[1]

Quite possibly the coolest night-lights in the world, these animals are injected with a glow-in-the-dark gene that is usually found in jellyfish. Scientists first began injecting the gene into fish in order to track their migration patterns but then moved on to more cuddly animals, including cats, dogs, mice, and rabbits.

Super Cows[2]

In 1990, the first genetically modified bull was altered to "humanize" the milk of its offspring by making the offspring's milk more similar in nutritional composition to human breast milk. Since then a whole new breed has been created, with cows that are more resistant to ailments like mad cow disease and udder infections—and they also happen to have huge muscles. The animals were bred as a food source; their creators say that the additional muscle provides more lean meat.

Hybrid Super Salmon[3]

First created by AquaBounty Technologies on Prince Edward Island, Canada, the fish were injected with a transgene that causes them to grow to maturity two to four times faster than nature intended. The resulting new species of fish, dubbed "advanced hybrid super salmon," could potentially end the need for expansive ocean farming of the species. However, hundreds of grocers refuse to sell the genetically altered fish in the interest of looking out for the health of their customers as well as the livelihood of salmon fishermen. To be honest, "advanced hybrid super salmon" is something I would rather see in a comic book than on my dinner plate.

Popeye Pigs[4]
Somehow, Japanese scientists found a way to genetically modify pigs by injecting them with a "spinach gene" that converts saturated fat into unsaturated fat, essentially transforming the pig into both meat and vegetable. However, critics argue that this hybrid is completely unnecessary, as you could simply eat your vegetables on the side. To those critics I would counter that bacon and bacon is tastier than bacon and veggies.

The Sudden-Death Mosquito[5]
A British firm called Oxitec has genetically engineered a new breed of insect that mates with regular mosquitos and subsequently produces offspring that can't survive until adulthood. Dubbed "sudden-death mosquitoes," these pests succeeded in reducing the mosquito population but critics complain that they have upset the ecosystem. Who cares? I hate mosquitoes!

Dolly the Sheep Clone[6]
Dolly is the crème de la crème of animal genetic mutation. Born out of a Scottish lab in 1996, she was the first mammal successfully cloned from an adult cell. She lived seven years before succumbing to a lung disease common in senior sheep. However, the amount of information extracted from both her creation and life has aided in the advancement of cellular research aimed at combatting diseases like Parkinson's.

The Craziest Drugs You Never Knew Existed

So, growing up we're all told by our teachers and parents to never do drugs because they're addictive (they'll ruin your life, baby), but the drugs that they warn us about are always the same old boring compounds. It's always the crack cocaine, the meth, and the devil weed. As dangerous as those drugs can be, they're nothing compared to the lesser-known drugs that are far stronger and have way scarier effects. Check these out. . . . I mean, DON'T EVER CHECK THESE OUT!

The Devil's Breath[7]

The drug, scopolamine, is known on the street as "the Devil's Breath" and can cause suggestibility and amnesia. The plant that it comes from is common in South America, which makes it common with Colombian criminals. The scariest part about Devil's Breath is that it is a completely odorless and tasteless powder that can simply be blown into a victim's face. The victim will then do anything the robber says—from emptying bank accounts to opening the front door of his or her own house. And the worst part is that the victim won't remember anything the next day. Good thing Devil's Breath isn't easily available in Canada. . . . Or is it?

DIPT[8]

This drug, Diisopropyltryptamine, is unique because unlike hallucinogenics that make you *see* crazy things, this one has completely auditory effects: hearing voices and distorted music, general confusion, and ringing in the ears that lasts up to two weeks. (I'm sorry, but exactly what part of that is supposed to be fun? Why would you want to take a drug that makes you feel like you've been at a concert for two weeks?)

Jenkem[9]

This one's made of poop! Also known as "butt hash," Jenkem is a hallucinogenic inhalant that's made from fermented human waste. It's popular among Zambian children, who store the dookie in a bottle for a week or so. The methane that forms in the bottle is inhaled, which creates visual and auditory hallucinations for about an hour. Users say that tripping on the drug makes them forget all of their worries and see visions. I don't care how cool the experience feels; I don't think I could ever get past the poop part.

> **FAN FACT: Studies suggest that sugar is more addicting than crack cocaine.**[10]
>
> —*Josh Sadoff, Eagan, Minn.*

DNP[11]

The drug 2,4-dinitrophenol, better known as DNP, is popularly taken for weight loss. Essentially what it does is severely ramp up your body's energy consumption, meaning that you could literally sit around all day eating burgers and fries and still lose a ton of weight. Sounds pretty good, right? Not exactly, because all of that energy use massively raises your body temperature, so much so that you essentially cook from the inside. Officially, this drug is discontinued; however, it is still widely available in online pharmacies. Friends, trust me, the best way to lose weight is to hit the gym.

> FAN FACT: In order to overdose on potassium, a person would have to eat roughly 480 bananas.[12]
>
> —*Ewan S., Great Britain*

Etorphine[13]

This drug works exactly like morphine and heroin, except it is three to five *thousand* times stronger. Primarily used to knock out large animals, it is so strong that .01 gram can knock out a large elephant. This drug is so crazy that simple contact with human skin will cause an overdose. It's available on the streets but it's not super popular, as you can imagine, because the biggest side effect is death. Interestingly, etorphine has been used in multiple TV shows, from *The Office* to *The Vampire Diaries* to *Dexter*. In fact, it was the drug that Dexter used every episode to knock out his victims. (Damn, Hollywood, you'd better be careful or you're gonna create some real-life psychos.)

Yage[14]

This drink is a psychedelic mix of various plants, including a South American vine that contains the compound dimethyltryptamine (DMT). It is said to be one of the most effective tools of enlightenment; those who consume it claim to experience profound positive changes in their lives afterward. Of course I'm not referring to the side effects of the drug, which include potentially losing your mind, explosive diarrhea, and intense vomiting (but don't let that scare you). Courtney Love is a huge proponent of this stuff . . . not exactly a ringing endorsement for the masses.

Krokodil[15]

This one has to be the nastiest drug on this list. Desomorphine, known on the street as Krokodil, is a cheap synthetic morphine that's made from codeine, iodine, and red phosphorous. It is essentially a brown sludge that has effects similar to heroin's, except it has way more serious side effects. The users of this drug develop severely dried-out skin that gets quickly eaten away by toxic ingredients. Disturbingly, that's where the drug gets its name—it leaves its victims looking like they've developed crocodile skin. SERIOUSLY, WHO WOULD EVER INJECT THIS STUFF?

Hopefully this chapter will convince you to NEVER DO DRUGS, kids. Get high on life instead. Mmmmkay?

THE MOST PAINFUL PASTIMES ON EARTH

SPORTS COACHES LOVE motivating players by talking about pain. "Play through the pain" is a popular mantra, along with "Pain is fear leaving the body" and "Pain is temporary; glory is forever." For the games in this chapter, however, expressions such as "It's not whether you get knocked down; it's whether you get back up" don't really apply because these sports are all about getting knocked down, kicked around, poked, pulled, and scared within an inch of your life. The crazy "athletes" who partake in the following pastimes don't simply tolerate pain; they pursue it.

Shin-Kicking Competition[1]
The marquee event of the Cotswold Olimpicks, the Shin-Kicking World Championships, is pretty straightforward: Two competitors take turns kicking each other in the shins until

one of them falls over. According to the website of the Olim-pick Games, the sport dates back hundreds of years. "In the early 19th Century the activity was more brutal, with villages challenging each other, contestants hardening shins with coal-hammers and wearing boots tipped with iron! Many a leg was broken!" Luckily, the stakes have softened since the 1800s, and today men are allowed to pad their shins with straw. Unfortunately, the straw shifts easily, leaving many competitors with defenseless shins. Even more unfortunate is the fact that victorious competitors are rewarded with more shin-kicking matches, until there is just one man left stand-ing. I don't think I'd ever participate in a sport that beckons would-be competitors with the tagline "Get the shin kicked out of you."

The Ear Pull[2]
The World Eskimo-Indian Olympics include a series of poten-tially painful contests such as the Arm Pull, Dropping the Bomb, and the Two-Foot High Kick. (I highly suggest binge-watching two-foot high kick videos on YouTube. I don't sug-gest trying to do it yourself.) However, the single-most painful event at the WEIO has got to be the Ear Pull. According to the WEIO website, the Ear Pull is "[a] game of stamina to pain, [in which] the victor demonstrates he/she can withstand pain, a trait sometimes needed to survive the harsh realities of the North. Two people will begin a 'tug-of-war' with their ears to see who the winner is." Basically, two competitors sit across from each other with a single loop of sinew wrapped around one of their ears (right to right, left to left). Without twisting

or jerking, they pull their heads straight back until the sinew is pulled off one competitor's ear or until someone gives up. Where do I sign up?

Competitive Eating[3]

Reading through the Records section of the Major League Eating website, I learned that Matt "the Megatoad" Stonie once ate 182 strips of Smithfield bacon in five minutes. Meanwhile, Sonya "the Black Widow" Thomas ate 8.4 pounds of baked beans in under three minutes in 2004. Eight and a half pounds of baked beans? That can't be safe for you (or anyone who walks behind you). In 2014, *Time* magazine ran an article called "Here's What Competitive Eating Does to Your Body," in which the author discusses how competitive eaters trick the satiety reflex, which would normally let a person know that he is full or that he needs to vomit. While the long-term effects of competitive eating are not yet known because the sport is relatively young, scientists predict that if the stomach is expanded beyond the point where it can return to its natural size, major surgery could be required to stem "intractable nausea and vomiting." I just looked up the word *intractable* and I'm out.

Noodling (a.k.a. Hillbilly Handfishin')[4]

Noodling is the sport of catching catfish using only one's hands. "Noodlers" reach into the dark and muddy riverbank lairs of the catfish and then try to bait the catfish into biting down on their hands. Did I mention that the fish are about three feet long and can weigh more than fifty pounds? Oh, and their bites have been described as "a rat trap with sandpaper." Did I also mention that the noodlers can't see the fish under the water and mud? They simply probe the holes and wait. Sounds crazy to me. Then again, so does the noodling strategy of (according to Smithsonian.com) "tossing junk, like large pipes and furniture, into lakes to provide catfish with nesting structure and themselves with an advantage in finding the fish when the nesting season comes."

Note: Noodling advocates are quick to point out that their sport doesn't seriously injure the catfish . . . unless the noodlers decide to eat them.

Penile Weight Lifting[5]

Gotta be honest, I had a tough time believing that this was actually a thing. However, extensive (unfortunate pun right there) googling has shown me that, in fact, lots of men across the world engage in the practice of lifting weights with their dongs. Some guys load up the willy weights as a means of increasing the size of their "little guy" (which doesn't work, by the way. Not that I tried it. . . . I just read about it. . . . I swear) while others train for competitions all over the world that I don't suggest you search for online unless you want your dreams haunted for the foreseeable future. Seriously, I don't get it. If I'm wearing loose shorts and the wind changes direction, I go down in a heap of pain. What do people get out of lifting rocks with their . . . y'know?

Whipping (by Choice)[6]

I don't get whipping. I know that a lot of religious people are into it (they call it self-flagellation), like the really pale guy in *The Da Vinci Code*, and a lot of freaky people are intrigued by it (as evidenced by the hundreds of millions of dollars that *Fifty Shades of Grey* made at the box office), but I just don't see the appeal. In 2009, an Opus Dei member spoke out on behalf of whipping, suggesting that people should "reconnect with their bodies and take control via moderate fasting and some corporal mortification, finding it a very healthy practice, which can overcome such unhealthy developments as drug use, sexual addictions, eating disorders and other body-hating approaches." So basically, Opus Dei was running a "Don't Hate, Just Hit" campaign. I'm not going to subscribe to that golden rule anytime soon.

Alligator Wrestling[7]

In 2010, the Seminole tribe of Florida founded the Freestyle Alligator Wrestling Championships, which was basically a rodeo with alligators. Come one, come all! Come risk losing a limb while earning almost no prize money! Do it for the adulation of a county fair full of rednecks. This chapter is making me think that I should make up my own sports league. I'm sure I could come up with something cooler than overeating or reptile wrestling. Hmmm . . . let me get back to you on that.

Snake Charming[8]

The practice of snake charming most likely began in ancient Egypt, though the charming style made popular in Hollywood movies like the Indiana Jones series likely stems from India. Regardless of where the activity comes from, however, there is little doubt that it takes a special type of crazy to do this full-time, which, by the way, is the only way anyone should charm snakes. Snake charming is not a part-time hobby. You either become an expert or you become dead. And even then the experts are in danger. In 2015, the *Daily Mail* wrote a story about the "Snake Prince" of Malaysia, who is famous for kissing king cobras on the lips, just as his father, the "Snake King," did before him. That is, until the Snake King died from a snakebite. Apparently ninety-nine career snakebites was one too many. Hey, at least snake charmers don't try to wrestle their reptiles. On the other hand, alligators aren't poisonous.

Proximity Flying[9]

I blame energy drinks for this one. You would have to be super jacked-up on sugar and caffeine to objectively look at the sport of wingsuit flying, in which people put on what essentially amounts to flying squirrel suits before throwing themselves off mountains, and think, "Man, that's just not dangerous or difficult enough on its own." Proximity flying is just like wingsuit flying except instead of jumping into open space and flying toward a large, open landing area, the goal is to fly close to buildings, objects, landmarks, or the ground. Let me repeat this: The goal is to jump off tall things without a parachute and then taunt death further by flying close to buildings. Sounds like fun, except the exact opposite.

The Beer Mile[10]

Scanning over the previous entries on this list, one would think that alcohol plays a role in motivating the "athletes" in at least half of these competitions (hopefully not snake charming or proximity flying) to participate. To that extent, several of the aforementioned activities could qualify as drinking games, except that the phrase "drinking games" has already been designated for those in which booze consumption is an element of the competition as opposed to simply a confidence booster. Long utilized as a weak justification for the poor decisions of university students, drinking games like Beer Pong and Flip Cup have lived outside the boundaries of legitimate sport, despite their adoption by hipster bars from Toronto to Tampa. However, in 2015 one drinking game broke through the barrier: the Beer Mile.

The Beer Mile is a relatively simple race. Competitors chug a beer before each quarter mile and the first person across the finish line wins. On August 23, 2015, runners/drinkers from all over the globe met in San Francisco to take part in the Beer Mile World Classic. ESPN covered the event, which was also the culmination of months of trash talk between the top runners/drinkers. Of the three favorites entering the men's competition, only one would actually complete the race. One favorite was disqualified for leaving too much beer in his cans and the other suffered a "reversal of fortune," meaning he threw up mid-race. At the end of the day, twenty-one-year-old Canadian Lewis Kent took home the trophy. Race organizers were thrilled with the event and predicted exponential growth for their "sport."

Personally, I would pay good money to watch the pay-per-view broadcast of a decathlon featuring all ten of these painful pastimes. What kind of person would it take to run a beer mile before jumping off a mountain into a river to wrestle an alligator before lifting junk with his junk, all while pounding ten kilograms of Twinkies? I want to meet the people who would be willing to tackle such an event. In fact, I want to worship them.

SPECIAL SECTION: JAPAN BLOWS MY MIND

JAPAN IS HOME to a disproportionate number of mind-blowing factoids, and assuming you didn't open up directly to this page, you likely have noticed Japan's influence on this book thus far. Similarly, any fan of my YouTube channels will notice that Japanese people, places, and things have become staples in my "Amazing Facts to Blow Your Mind" lists. Given Japan's special place in my heart, I felt it was only appropriate to dedicate a special section to the Land of the Rising Sun.

Here are some of Japan's most entertaining offbeat characters, stories, and traditions.

Houshi—the Hotel That Has Been Run by 46 Generations of the Same Family[1]

Houshi is a traditional Japanese inn and spa in Komatsu, Japan, that has the distinction of being the second-oldest hotel in the world, having opened its doors after a Buddhist monk envisioned the spa's hot springs in a dream almost thirteen hundred years ago, in 718 AD! More impressive than the inn's longevity, however, is the fact that the same family has managed it the entire thirteen hundred years. No, the innkeepers are not immortal spa vampires (though that would be amazing). Rather, the family has passed its business from generation to generation an astonishing forty-five times (and you thought that your family barbecues were a long-standing tradition). The family traces its ancestry back to a Buddhist monk in the seventh century who adopted a boy and named him Zengoro. Every firstborn son has since taken the same name and then taken over the family business. The current owner of the spa is the forty-sixth Zengoro! Unfortunately, the forty-seventh Zengoro passed away in 2013, which means that his little sister is poised to become the first female innkeeper once her parents retire, thereby adding a new layer to the family tradition.

Serious Pinky Swears[2]

In Japan, the roots of the pinky swear can be traced back hundreds of years, when the gesture meant that if one of the promisers happened to break her promise, she would be forced to cut off her pinky. North American teenage girls take note, pinky swears are not to be taken lightly!

Owl Cafés[3]

Japan is full of animal-themed restaurants. However, unlike Canada or the United States, these eateries aren't just decorated with animal pictures and fake habitats. Instead they are full of live animals that patrons can play with as they drink their lattes. Is it sanitary? Doubtful. This definitely wouldn't *fly* with North American health inspectors. Is it awesome? Heck yes, it's awesome. There are all kinds of animal cafés in Tokyo alone—cat cafés, dog cafés, lizard cafés, parrot cafés, and more. I think the coolest, however, are the owl cafés. Who doesn't want to eat a pastry while a great horned owl sits on your head? Don't even get me started on the role-playing possibilities for Harry Potter fans.

Bonus Fact: Tashirojima, or Cat Island, is an island in Japan where stray cats outnumber people.

Our Lady of Akita[4]

Located near the town of Akita in Northern Honshu, a famous statue of the Virgin Mary has gone through several events that were beyond weird. On July 6, 1978, nuns heard a voice coming from the statue in the chapel where it resides. On the same day, the same sisters noticed drops of blood flowing from a wound on the statue's hand. Shortly afterward, the wounds disappeared but the statue began sweating from its forehead and neck. Two years later, on January 4, the statue began to weep, which it continued to do in intervals for almost seven years! The most interesting thing about these events is that a scientific analysis of all the blood, sweat, and tears from the statue confirmed that they were all from a real human. Now, I'm sure that this story provides lots of hope for religious people, but if that was me and I saw liquid coming out of a statue, I would sprint out the door and probably knock over a few old ladies on the way. It would not be good.

Lala, the Penguin That Went Shopping for Fish[5]
Back in the 1980s, Yukio Nishimoto, a construction manager in the southern town of Shibushi, Japan, commented how much he liked his buddy's stuffed penguin. A while later, while fishing somewhere in the Indian Ocean his friend noticed a live penguin with a badly injured back and decided to bring it home to Japan for Nishimoto. The fisherman assumed the penguin would die, which would allow Nishimoto to have a stuffed penguin of his own. Here's the thing, though: The penguin, who Nishimoto named Lala (technically Rara), didn't die. Instead the Nishimotos nursed the penguin back to health and treated him like a son. They built him his own small enclosed bedroom with a massive air conditioner and they taught him how to walk into town and visit the fish market. Every day Lala would throw on his small backpack and waddle down the road, stopping by the neighbor's house to take a shower with the hose, and then hitting the store for some mackerel or sardines (his favorite). The *Real TV* report on Lala that ran in the late 1990s is one of my favorite videos on the Internet.

Chocolate Legos[6]

For years, Japanese designer Akihiro Mizuuchi and his friends had a Valentine's Day tradition—they would build re-creations of characters from their favorite robot anime cartoon, *Mobile Suit Gundam*, out of chocolate. Presumably tired of making dumpy and melty-looking Hershey's robots, Mizuuchi decided to step up his chocolate Gundam game by designing a modular system for manufacturing edible chocolate Lego bricks, which he then used to blow his friends' minds on Valentine's Day. In typical Japanese fashion, he also used the bricks to make cute yet slightly creepy animal figures. The real question is, did Mizuuchi's invention help him land a girlfriend? Alas, I couldn't find the answer on the Internet. Regardless, his invention was a breakthrough for people all over the world who want to be creative and obese at the same time!

> FAN FACT: Ronald McDonald is known as Donald McDonald in Japan. In Singapore he's known as Uncle McDonald.[7]   —*Nicolette Y., Waco, Tex.*

Okinawa—the Healthiest Place on Earth[8]

As of 2010, there were over 400 people in Okinawa who were at least 100 years old. By 2030, estimates project that there will be more than 200,000 centenarians living on the island. According to the Okinawa Centenarian Study, good genes are largely responsible for the population's longevity, but diet, exercise, and a "stress-minimizing psycho-spiritual outlook" also play a big role. Basically, Okinawans drink less, eat right, and chill out.

The Predator Shield Game[9]

Japanese game shows are known for being over the top and completely ridiculous and every time I think they may have run out of ideas, a clip from a show like *Sekai No Hatte Madde Itte Q!* shows up online with a game called Predator Shield and completely restores my faith in the demented brains of Japanese game show producers. Predator Shield is a pretty straightforward concept. Contestants climb into a glass box, which serves as their only shield against the large, terrifying animal of the week that tries like hell to open or break the box and then eat said contestants. In the clip I saw online, the predator in question was a giant grizzly bear and the woman in the box couldn't stop screaming. Here's the crazy part: Watching the clip, as this poor woman was being batted around in this see-through cube, screaming herself hoarse as her life passed before her eyes, I couldn't stop laughing and I have no idea why. Those producers are geniuses.

The Vanishing Underwater Roller Coaster[10]

I don't think a whole lot needs to be said about this one. At Yokohama Cosmo World there is an amazing roller coaster that takes riders into an underwater tunnel. For people watching the ride from the rest of the park, the roller coaster seems to completely vanish into the sea like a submarine. Pretty cool.

Legendary Ninjas[11]

As cool as the underwater roller coaster is, it is totally lame compared to legendary Japanese ninjas. Take, for example, the legend of Hattori Hanzo, the most famous ninja of them all. Hanzo was a master spear fighter and swordsman who was said to have supernatural abilities. He protected the shogun, he may or may not have been able to disappear and reappear like a ghost, and he is said to have founded an undercover agency of ninjas. *Undercover ninja agency!* AAAAAHH!

Here lies Matt. His brain just exploded.

Legendary Human[12]

On August 6, 1945, Tsutomu Yamaguchi was a twenty-nine-year-old engineer on the last day of a business trip in Hiroshima, Japan. He was walking through a company shipyard when an American B-29 bomber dropped the nuclear bomb on the city. The shockwave from the bomb tossed Yamaguchi into the air and nearly knocked him out. He had burns all over his arms and face and his eardrums ruptured. After spending the next couple of days in the midst of unspeakable destruction, Yamaguchi boarded a train for his hometown of Nagasaki. On August 9, he was in his boss's office, telling him about the Hiroshima bombing, when the Americans dropped the second nuclear bomb. Not only did Yamaguchi survive both bombings, but he went on to live past the age of ninety.

Part 3

THAT CAN'T BE TRUE, CAN IT?

TEN CRAZY
REAL-WORLD
DOPPELGÄNGERS

A DOPPELGÄNGER IS a "ghostly double or counterpart of a living person."[1] However, in popular culture the term is thrown around loosely to describe any two people who look similar but are not related. When I go out to get coffee and the barista tells me that I look like the guy from the *Transporter* movies, she is saying that Jason Statham is my doppelgänger. (*Note:* I look nothing like Jason Statham. This is an egregious example of "bald-ism.") When I began researching doppelgängers, I found some amazing human look-alikes, but I also started noticing uncanny resemblances between cities, cultures, animals, and gods. Several of these similarities extend well beyond coincidental looks, which makes me wonder if cosmic forces were at work in sculpting these twins across time and space.

Ancient Civilization Doppelgängers:[2]
The Incas and the Egyptians

Here are the facts. The ancient Egyptians and Incas evolved on opposite sides of the planet (Africa and South America, respectively). Although both civilizations developed groundbreaking technologies, neither was anywhere close to creating the Internet, cameras, phones, or telegraphs, which means that there was no way one civilization could check out what the other was up to and then knock off their culture. How then, were the accomplishments of the two civilizations so eerily similar? Both made pyramids out of stone. Both were into mummifying the dead, and the really important dead people in both cultures were buried with gold masks. Both based religions on the sun and built three doors onto the front of their temples. Also one can't help but notice that both cultures were obsessed with phallic symbolism. Bottom line: Long before celebrities had doppelgängers, civilizations had doppelgängers.

City Doppelgängers:[3] Paris and Tianducheng

Recognizing how expensive it is to travel all the way from Asia to Paris, real estate developers in Hangzhou, China, decided to build a clone of the City of Lights, named Tianducheng, in the middle of their country. The Chinese developers went all out, building models of popular landmarks like the Eiffel Tower and the fountain in the Gardens of Versailles. However, unlike the Paris-themed knockoffs in North America (Las Vegas, Epcot Center, etc.), which feature restaurants and theater shows, allowing vacationers the opportunity to have a Parisian experience for a few hours or days, Tianducheng offers

Chinese people the opportunity to *live* in fake Paris. The development has cobblestone streets, horse-drawn carriages, Parisian chapels, and enough Parisian-looking buildings to accommodate ten thousand residents. Unfortunately, developers grossly overestimated the number of people who would want to live in fake Paris. As of the writing of this book, the development is pretty much empty. On the bright side, it is a popular wedding destination. Themed weddings are a little less of a commitment than themed lives. However, that is not to say that building Paris's doppelgänger in the middle of China was a completely ridiculous idea, because there are similar Chinese knockoffs of Austrian and Italian cities that have proven to be more financially viable.

Planet Doppelgängers:[4] Earth and Kepler-452b

In 2015, NASA's Kepler satellite made a groundbreaking discovery that was sure to delight philosophers, filmmakers, and RV-driving New Mexicans: a new planet, called Kepler-452b, that is an "earthlike cousin." As Kepler researcher Jon Jenkins said, "The earth is a little less lonely because there's a new kid on the block and he moved in just right next door." I don't know what neighborhood Jon Jenkins grew up in but the blocks must have been huge because Kepler-452b is fourteen hundred light-years away. KepB (every new kid needs a nickname) has a lot of similarities to Earth, starting with the fact that it orbits a star that is a lot like our sun every 385 days. KepB is 1.6 times the size of Earth and has a stronger gravitational pull, but given its composition and atmospheric makeup, it appears to be the most Earthlike planet scientists have found to date.

Action Star Doppelgängers:[5] Bruce Willis and Gen. Douglas MacArthur

There are very few things that get the Internet as hot and bothered as a good historical figure–contemporary celebrity doppelgänger pairing. Whether it's Vincent van Gogh scowling like Chuck Norris or Shia LaBeouf flashing his pouty eyes like a young Albert Einstein, we love pop culture reincarnations. That said, the true gems of the genre match not only looks but also skills, which is why my favorite celebrity-history pairing is Bruce Willis and Gen. Douglas MacArthur, action stars of movie theater and military theater, respectively. Get this: MacArthur is best known as a World War II general who won the battle against Germany by securing Japanese territory (he was the supreme commander of the Southwest Pacific). Bruce Willis, meanwhile, is best known for playing John McClane, who successfully defeats a diabolical German (Hans Gruber) while securing Japanese territory (Nakatomi Plaza in Los Angeles) in the first *Die Hard* movie. McClane and MacArthur are basically brothers from another mother, right?

> FAN FACT: There are roughly seven people in the world who look exactly like you and there is a 9 percent chance you will run into one of them in your lifetime![6]
>
> —*Anas H., San Romanoway, Toronto, Ontario, Canada*

Goddess Doppelgängers:[7] Nephele and Hera

According to Greek mythology, Zeus created a doppelgänger of one of his wives, Hera, in order to trap a mortal king, Ixion, who had tried to hit on her at a party. Zeus created the cloud nymph Nephele by molding some clouds to look exactly like his wife, and Ixion took the bait hook, line, and sinker. He then forced himself on Nephele and as a result, she ended up giving birth to the father of the centaurs. Well, that was all the proof Zeus needed to see. He was so upset with Ixion that he chained the guy to a fiery wheel for all of eternity. No means no, bro. No means no. Meanwhile, benevolent god that he was, Zeus kept his wife's doppelgänger around and even made her the goddess of hospitality.

Spirit Doppelgängers:[8] Ka and the Story of Helen of Troy

Sticking with mythical doppelgängers based in lust, ancient Egyptian mythology tells an interesting version of the Trojan War that prominently features a spirit doppelgänger, or *ka*. The Egyptian version of the story begins just like the Greek version: The Trojan War started when the Trojan prince Paris swiped Helen, the most beautiful woman on earth, away from her husband, the King of Sparta. The king responded by bringing his army to Troy and assaulting the place for the next ten years before finally winning the war and taking his wife home. Now this is where the Egyptian story gets interesting, because while the Greek version says that Helen and the king lived (relatively) happily ever after, the Egyptian version suggests that the Helen who boarded the ships with her victorious husband wasn't real! She was merely a spirit double conjured up by the gods. The King of Sparta fought for ten years over a doppelgänger!

Animal Doppelgängers:[9] Shiba Inu and Fox

Not gonna get too complicated with this one. The Shiba Inu is a dog that looks like a fox. It looks so much like a fox, in fact, that one Shiba owner created a website for his dog with the address imnotafox.com. With bold personalities, strong minds, and hunting roots, Shibas act a lot like foxes as well, which is why stuffed animal–seeking Etsy surfers should be cautious before ordering Shiba Inu pups from a breeder. According to the website dogtime.com, "It is important to understand the freethinking nature of the Shiba Inu so you won't be frustrated. The Shiba Inu is highly intelligent, but he doesn't necessarily want to do what you want him to do. You may have to make him think obedience is his idea." Funny, several of my married friends describe their relationships the same way.

Warrior Doppelgängers:[10] Achilles and Yao Ming

This is my final mythology-driven doppelgänger, I promise. That said, this one is a time traveler and it was simply too good to keep out of the chapter. While I was researching the Helen of Troy spirit double, Achilles, the greatest warrior from the Trojan War, kept popping up, and as procrastinators often do, I got distracted from my primary assignment. But lucky for you I chased Achilles down the mental rabbit hole, or I never would have realized that his doppelgänger is none other than former Chinese basketball star Yao Ming. Stay with me on this one. Both Achilles and Yao Ming are the product of remarkable parents. Achilles's father was a king and his mother was immortal, which meant that their son was semi-divine and had greater strength and skill than mere mortals. Yao Ming, meanwhile, was born to parents who were both incredibly tall and were both prominent players in the Chinese basketball program. When Yao was born it was immediately apparent that he had been blessed with superhuman size (he would eventually grow to be seven feet six inches). Both Achilles and Yao Ming earned great accolades for their performance on their respective battlefields and both men had their careers cut short in their primes by unfortunate foot injuries. Reincarnation at work? You decide.

Grammatical Doppelgängers:[11] Homonyms

The words *bowl* and *bowl* may look exactly the same but, like celebrity doppelgängers, they are merely superficial lookalikes. One bowl holds breakfast cereal or soup, while the other is the act of rolling a heavy ball toward ten wooden pins. Homonyms are spelled the same and pronounced the same, yet have different definitions. Words that sound the same but are spelled differently, like *flower* and *flour*, are called homophones, while words that are spelled the same but sound different, like *bass* the fish and *bass* the instrument, are called homographs. Therefore the sentence "Upon learning I would soon be bald, I fell flat on the floor of my flat and bawled, then I moped for a while before joining a gym and buying a moped" contains a homophone, homonym, and a homograph!

Meat Doppelgängers:[12] Chicken and Snake

"Tastes like chicken" is the most overused descriptor for the taste of exotic flesh. However, several experts agree that one alterna-meat actually does taste like chicken, even if the texture is a little different: snake meat. According to a *Slate* article from 2012 on the subject, modern snakes are related to chickens through a group of animals called diapsids, which originated three hundred million years ago. As the author of that article says, "You wouldn't mistake the texture of snake for chicken, but run it through a meat-grinder, and you wouldn't know the difference." In 2013, the *Huffington Post* ran an infographic suggesting that animals that taste like chicken share several traits, including the fact that many of these animals come from eggs, are hunted by predators, and build homes underground. Makes me wonder why no enterprising entrepreneurs have launched Kentucky Fried Snake restaurants. Seems like there's a hole in the marketplace. Just sayin' . . .

REAL CHINESE SUPERSTITIONS AND FAKE CANADIAN SUPERSTITIONS

CHINA HAS MORE people, more written history, and more legends than any other country on earth, so it only makes sense that there is also a wealth of amazing superstitions. Many Chinese superstitions are rooted in fate and luck, and unlike most Western cultures, the Chinese do not assume that people have complete control over their fate. Instead, they believe that there are a number of outside influencers affecting fate, including actions committed in previous lives and incarnations.

The following is a list of amazing Chinese superstitions as well as some potential Canadian superstitions (that I made up).

REAL CHINESE SUPERSTITION: Clipping your toenails at night will allow ghosts and evil spirits to come into your house.[1] Also, hide your toenails when you are done clipping them. This will prevent others from using them to cast spells on you or put curses on you. Come to think of it, whenever I leave my toenails out in the open after clipping them, my girlfriend curses me. . . .

FAKE CANADIAN SUPERSTITION: *Clipping your toenails with a Swiss Army knife will allow the infection fairy to enter your hunting cabin.*

REAL CHINESE SUPERSTITION: **Green hats mean your wife is cheating on you.**[2] In China, green hats are a symbol of adultery. One explanation for this is that the Chinese translation of the phrase "wearing a green hat" sounds similar to the Chinese translation of *cuckold* (the husband of a cheater). Another story is that families of prostitutes in the Yuan dynasty were forced to wear green hats. A third explanation suggests that brothel workers during the Tang dynasty wore green hats (by the way, "Brothel Workers of the Tang Dynasty" sounds like the title of an amazing reality show). My question is, what happens if you wear an Irish hat with a four-leaf clover on it in Beijing? Which juju wins out?

FAKE CANADIAN SUPERSTITION: *Wearing a hockey jersey at your wedding means that your wife will soon be cheating on you.*

REAL CHINESE SUPERSTITION: **Mustaches are unlucky.**[3] In this case, the Chinese are simply telling us what single hipsters have known for years—nobody gets lucky with a crazy mustache. In fact, in China the dirty caterpillar under your nose actually symbolizes bad luck and misfortune. Well-groomed facial hair is not quite as unlucky but that doesn't mean it's worth growing.

FAKE CANADIAN SUPERSTITION: Mullets are lucky . . . but only at Nickelback concerts.

REAL CHINESE SUPERSTITION: If you cage a turtle and keep it as a pet it will ruin your business by slowing it down.[4] Contrast this with Japan, where if you feed your turtle radioactive ooze, teach it to skateboard, and feed it pizza, it might save your city from Shredder.

FAKE CANADIAN SUPERSTITION: If you allow your pet bear to sleep in your bed, it will ruin your breathing by slowing it down or stopping it entirely.

REAL CHINESE SUPERSTITION: If a pregnant woman cries, her baby will be a whiny mess its whole life.[5] Hey, pregnant ladies, I know that your emotions are swirling like a hurricane and a change in the wind can make you depressed, but you'd better shut off the waterworks or your child will be haunted. Also, a baby crying for no good reason means that there are ghosts flying around the child, which is another reason to suck it up and smile. Also, don't use glue (difficult labor), push a stroller (bad luck), let people rub your belly (spoiled child), or use curse words (your baby will be cursed). These add a whole new dimension to the nature versus nurture debate.

FAKE CANADIAN SUPERSTITION: If you tell a pregnant woman to suck it up and smile, you will begin to feel intense pain in your crotch.

REAL CHINESE SUPERSTITION: The number 4 is bad, but 8 is great. One study found that in a North American community with a large immigrant population, houses with an address that ended in 4 sold for an average of 2.2 percent less than houses with other addresses. Meanwhile, addresses that ended with 8 went for a 2.5 percent premium.[6]

FAKE CANADIAN SUPERSTITION: Even if the hockey jersey you wear at your wedding has the number 8 on the back, your spouse will cheat on you.

REAL CHINESE SUPERSTITION: Decline a gift three times before accepting. Similarly, if someone refuses you three times, you should keep insisting until they say yes.[7]

FAKE CANADIAN SUPERSTITION: When presented with a double dare, you should down three beers before accepting. Similarly, if someone refuses your double dare, you should taunt him or her mercilessly into acceptance.

CHINESE NEW YEAR SUPERSTITIONS[8]

- DON'T cut your noodles on New Year's Day because New Year's noodles are a symbol of long life. Don't get a haircut either (same reason). Actually, you should probably stay away from knives and scissors in general on New Year's, lest you risk your long life by cutting *anything*.

- DO shoot off firecrackers, as that is a symbol of launching the old and welcoming the new. In China, fireworks and noisemakers are believed to scare away evil spirits.[9]
- DON'T sweep or dust on New Year's, or you run the risk of sweeping away your good fortune. (What happens if someone gets sick at your New Year's Eve party? Do you leave the "lucky" mess on the carpet?)
- DO be nice to the first person you see on New Year's Day, as you will help ensure his or her good fortune for the rest of the year.
- DON'T buy books.[10] In Cantonese, *book* is a homonym for *lose*, which is why Chinese bookstores are closed on New Year's Day.
- DO pay your bills, because the Chinese believe that if you start the year as a moocher, you'll end the year as a moocher. Similarly, don't lend money, because you'll be lending all year. Also, make sure to use crisp new bills, because they are symbols of good luck.
- DON'T cry on New Year's Day because—you guessed it—that means you'll be crying for the rest of the year.

BONUS FACTS!

- Every panda in the world is owned by China. If you happen to see one outside the country, it is simply on loan.[11]
- If the population of China walked by you single file, the line would never end because of the rate of reproduction.[12]

FAST FACTS

More Powerful Than You Think

- A single search on Google takes more computing power than it did to land *Apollo 11* on the moon.[1]
- Microwaves use more electricity to power their clocks than to heat up your food.[2]
- Human bone is four times as strong as concrete (which is part of the reason that humans are not appropriate prey for great white sharks, because shark digestion is too slow to cope with the high ratio of bone to muscle and fat).[3]
- Falling coconuts kill fifteen times as many people as shark attacks do every year.[4]

> **FAN FACT: Your stomach acid can dissolve metal.**[5]
>
> *—Jack Murray, New York*

- A grizzly bear's jaws are so strong that its bite could crush a bowling ball. Also, its sense of smell is so acute that it can travel eighteen miles straight to a food source.[6]

> **FAN FACT: Our hearts create enough pressure to squirt blood thirty feet.**[7]
>
> *—Caytlynn J., Tulsa, Okla.*

- A honeybee can lift three hundred times its own weight.[8]
- The sun is roughly 27,000,000 degrees Fahrenheit at its core.[9]
- In 2015, British researchers determined that the microscopic teeth of small sea snails called limpets are made of the strongest natural substance in the world.[10] The researchers believe that humans could adapt the snail's technology to design better planes, boats, and dental fillings. The previous title holder for nature's strongest substance was spider silk.

HISTORICAL WIZARDS AND THEIR SWAG RANKINGS

SOMETIMES REAL CHARACTERS from history are more magical and mysterious than any of the characters you could read about in a book or see in a movie. Such is the case when it comes to the amazing wizards who actually existed. From the Yin-Yang Master to the Voodoo Queen of New Orleans, the legendary powers of the magical women and men from history range from the impressive to the astounding.

"But who was the most powerful wizard of all time?" you ask. To help answer that question, I have allotted one hundred points to each wizard across multiple skill categories in order to offer a more complete assessment of their individual might. These ratings comprise each sorcerer's SWAG (Santoro Wizard Ability Grade).

Abe no Seimei, the Yin-Yang Master,[1] is often referred to as the Japanese Merlin, a nod to the famous sorcerer from King Ar-

thur's court. The life of Abe no Seimei was well chronicled because he served six different emperors, performing duties that ranged from analyzing strange events to predicting the future to banishing illness and evil spirits. He was called a yin-yang master, which might be the best possible nickname ever for a sorcerer (or for a bald Canadian rapper. Hmm . . .). Some suggested that one of Abe no Seimei's parents was actually a fox, that he had the ability to see demons, and that he could will objects to change their shape. He was so memorable, in fact, that the mystical equidistant five-pointed star, known as a pentagram in the West, is called a Seiman in Japan, the seal of Abe no Seimei.

SWAG	
INTELLIGENCE	25
SUMMONING SPIRITS	25
SHAPE-SHIFTING	35
INTIMIDATION	10

Rasputin[2] Grigori Rasputin was a trusted faith healer and friend to the Tsar of Russia in the early twentieth century. He is known for his mystical abilities and also for the difficulty assassins faced when trying to kill him. Like many sorcerers throughout history, Rasputin was feared and demonized by the mortals he served. In his case, the Russian public blamed him for the country's failures in World War I, and the powers that be decided to take him out. First they poisoned him, but he would not die. Next, they shot him, but he still didn't die. Only after poisoning, shooting, and drowning Rasputin in the same night were assassins able to take him out.

SWAG	
CHARM	6
CREEPY LOOKS	10
HEALING POWER	70

Dee and Kelley[3] These two Renaissance occultists (practitioners of mystical, supernatural, or magical activities) were the original magical odd couple. Dee was a magical practitioner who dedicated his life to spiritual experimentation, alchemy, and astrology. He was an adviser to the Queen of England on astrological and scientific matters in the middle of the sixteenth century. Kelley, on the other hand, was a rogue, a former alchemist who became obsessed with the idea of turning cheap metals into gold. In fact, when the two met, Kelley was using an alias, "Talbot," to mask a former forgery conviction. That said, Kelley so impressed Dee with his crystal-gazing skills that the two spent the next several years communicating with angels and pursuing the philosopher's stone (several centuries before Harry Potter and his sorcerer's stone), which was said to have the power to turn metal to gold and/or grant immortality.

SWAG	
CRYSTAL GAZING	50
ALCHEMY	10
TEAMWORK	20
IMMORTALITY	0

The Maharal of Prague[4] Rabbi Judah Loew ben Bezalel was the chief rabbi in Prague (then the center of the European Jewish community) around the turn of the seventeenth century. He was a very accomplished scholar, spiritual leader, and scientist. That said, nobody remembers the accomplishments of your day job when you're the guy who created the supernatural monster that protects your people from the Roman Empire. As legend has it, the Jews of Prague were being unfairly blamed for several societal issues, natural catastrophes, and other unfortunate events over which they had no involvement or control. The threat of expulsion, mob violence, and false imprisonment had everyone a little freaked out. Rabbi Loew, recognizing that his people stood no chance against a crazed Roman mob, went down to the river and formed a man-shaped monster out of clay, a golem, to protect his people. The golem went to the entrance of the Jewish ghetto and proceeded to demolish the first wave of the angry Roman mob. The rest of the mob didn't want any part of the clay monster, so they just turned and ran.

SWAG	
SURPRISE	5
MONSTER CONTROL	70
BREAKDANCING	0
LEADERSHIP	15

Magician of Marblehead[5] Edward Dimond lived around the time of the Salem witch trials in the 1690s, in the seaside town of Marblehead, Massachusetts. As a boy, Edward frequently went into "trances" in which he would neither sleep nor eat yet when he emerged he would feel refreshed. As he grew older, his trances were accompanied by magical visions of the past and future. He was often sought out to help solve crimes or locate lost items; many of the townspeople were thankful that he was willing to share his gifts. However, Dimond allegedly had a much darker side as well. When bad storms approached, he would walk into the middle of the cemetery and howl at the wind. Ship captains at sea reported hearing Dimond's voice during the storms. Sometimes the voice would tell them how to plot courses to avoid the weather; other times, when ships were captained by his enemies, Dimond would instruct the storm to sink the vessels. What's the moral here? Don't bully the kid who goes into trances!

SWAG	
MAGICAL VISIONS	30
WEATHER MANIPULATION	20
TRANCE REGENERATION	30
FORGIVENESS	3

The Voodoo Queen of New Orleans[6] Most voodoo practitioners in New Orleans practice one of two kinds of magic: white or black. White magic is positive. A love potion, for example, is white magic. Black magic, on the other hand, is dark and potentially deadly. There is, however, a third kind of magic in New Orleans as well, drawing from both black magic and white magic and more powerful than both. This gray magic is called "gris-gris" (taken from the French word for *gray*). The most famous gris-gris practitioner in the history of New Orleans was Marie Laveau. She was born around 1800, the child of a Creole mother and African American father. Marie had two children, both of whom died young and mysteriously, as did her first husband. She then became a high-society hairdresser, which gave her rare access to the secrets of the socialites and their slaves. When she became a voodoo queen in the 1830s, she leveraged her knowledge of both spells and secrets to make magic happen and quickly became the biggest power broker in all of New Orleans. Today, Marie Laveau's legacy still shines bright in New Orleans as products and businesses bearing her name are the first choice for French Quarter fortune seekers, those looking to hex an enemy, and lovers in need of passion potions. Also, the cemetery in which she is buried is rumored to be haunted.

SWAG	
VOODOO	50
LISTENING	20
FORTUNE-TELLING	10
HEXES	10

Nostradamus[7] is the most famous prophet of all time, rumored to have predicted (among other events) the French Revolution, Napoléon, Hitler, the atomic bomb, and the deaths of multiple monarchs. After starting his career as a healer, Nostradamus began publishing his prophecies at a prolific rate. In fact he is said to have published more than six thousand vaguely dated and worded predictions. While his successful predictions are legendary, I wonder how accurate Nostradamus was overall. I mean, in addition to predicting wars and assassinations, did he also predict that dogs would learn to talk?

SWAG	
PREDICTING	90
EDITING	2
ACCURACY	2

Paracelsus[8] was born in 1493 with the most magical name of anyone on this list: Philippus Aureolus Theophrastus Bombastus von Hohenheim. His name is as long as a full magic spell! The son of a famous physician, Paracelsus introduced advanced alchemy to the fields of medicine and surgery. He also named the element zinc in 1526. However, the reason Paracelsus is on this list is because he created the Alphabet of the Magi, a series of magical symbols that he engraved on talismans, intended to summon the angels to heal the sick.

SWAG	
IMPRESSIVE NAME	30
HEALING	12
ALCHEMY	20
ANGEL SUMMONING	24

Hew Draper, the Wizard Who Claimed He Wasn't[9] When sixteenth-century British innkeeper Hew Draper was sent to the Tower of London for attempted sorcery, he swore up and down that he wasn't into the occult. Sure, he used to have some magical books, but he burned those a long time ago, he claimed. However, Draper's "I'm not the wizard you think I am" defense took a major hit when he got bored in prison and decided to carve a detailed astrological sphere, complete with all kinds of zodiacal tags, into the stone wall of the tower. He then *signed the artwork* and promptly disappeared. Nobody knows whether Draper escaped from the tower, died there, or beamed himself to another dimension.

SWAG	
ASTROLOGY	40
ESCAPE ARTISTRY	40
LYING	0

Michael Scot, the Scottish Wizard,[10] was a thirteenth-century European wizard. By this point in the list we should all recognize that alchemy, astrology, and astronomy were prerequisite courses for a sorcery degree during this time period, and Scot had all of them covered. We should also have learned by now that there was no better way to build your wizard reputation than by curing an ailing ruler, which is what Scot did for the Holy Roman emperor, Frederick II. Once his street cred was built up, the Scottish Wizard felt comfortable carrying out all sorts of otherworldly tasks for His Majesty, including predicting the outcomes of wars and calculating the distance between the top of the church and heaven. After his death, Scot's legend continued to grow as storytellers remembered him as a man who carried a magic staff and used witchcraft to fight pirates. I'm ready for Johnny Depp to star in the Michael Scot biopic.

WITCHCRAFT	20
HEALING	20
STAFF FIGHTING	40

....

And the winner, with a 95 SWAG rating, is . . . **Abe no Seimei**! Of all the impressive achievements on this list, it's hard to dispute the dominance of a sorcerer whose reputation reached across the oceans and earned him not one but two world-class nicknames: Japanese Merlin and Yin-Yang Master.

FAST FACTS

Word!

- *Overmorrow* is an actual word that means "the day after tomorrow."[1]

> FAN FACT: A buttload is an actual measurement, equal to roughly 126 gallons.[2]
> —*Brooke H., Hamilton, Ontario, Canada*

- The Hawaiian alphabet has only twelve letters: a, e, i, o, u, h, k, l, m, n, p, w[3]

> FAN FACT: If you spell out every number in order, you won't see the letter *a* until one thousand.[4]
> —*Sofia B., United States*

- The typical lead pencil can draw a line that is thirty-five miles long.[5]

> FAN FACT: *Facetiously* contains all five vowels and *y* in alphabetical order.[6]   —*Nikita Lorimer, New Zealand*

- *Sahara* is an Arabic word that means "great desert,"[7] which means that people who say "Sahara desert" are actually saying "Great Desert desert."

> FAN FACT: Hippopotomonstrosesquippedaliophobia is the fear of long words.   —*Elie Chase, Oregon*

- The word *verb* is actually a noun.

> FAN FACT: *Dreamt* is the only English word that ends in *mt*.[8]   —*Haley W., Philadelphia, Pa.*

- The dot over the lowercase *i* and *j* is called a "tittle."[9]

> FAN FACT: The combination of the letters *ough* can be pronounced ten different ways.[10]
> —*Ishaan C., Bangalore, India*

- There is no word in the English language that rhymes with *purple*, *orange*, or *silver*.[11]

> FAN FACT: The word *astronaut* comes from the
> Greek word *astron*, which means "star," and *nautes*,
> which means "sailor." The Russian *cosmonaut* has a
> similar meaning, from *kosmos*, meaning "universe,"
> and again *nautes* is a sailor. (So astronauts are
> Sailor Moon for anime fans.)[12]
> —*Conor Murtagh, London, United Kingdom*

- Oxford University Press, which publishes the *Oxford English Dictionary*, chooses a Word of the Year every year. Past winners include *vape* (2014), *selfie* (2013), *unfriend* (2009), and *podcast* (2005).[13]
- William Shakespeare is widely considered to be one of the greatest writers of all time, if not the greatest, but did you know that he was also a hip-hop pioneer? Consider the following:
    - He added seventeen hundred words to the English language, including *newfangled*, *bedazzled*, and *swagger*.[14]
    - He was the first person to use the letter *u* as a substitute for the word *you*, in his comedy *Love's Labour's Lost*, around 1595.[15]

If you want to dive deeper into this rabbit hole, I recommend checking out a 2012 TED talk from Akala, one of the members of the Hip Hop Shakespeare Company.[16]

YOUTUBE CHANNEL REMIX

The Creepiest Urban Legends That Turned Out to Be True (and the Movies That Should Be Based on Them)

SO WE'VE ALL heard an urban legend at some point in our lives. These stories seem to be designed for a specific reason: to scare the crap out of people. But what happens if the story isn't just a story? As it turns out, some of the most well-known urban legends aren't legends at all. In this chapter, I have gathered up the most disturbing urban legends to share with you, and as a bonus, I have summarized the feature films I would like to see based on each creepy tale.

The Body in the Wall[1] This urban legend says that while renovating a home, a construction worker knocks down a wall only to find a bare-bones skeleton staring back at him. Well, in 2011 while renovating the second floor of the Abbeville National Bank in Louisiana, workers discovered in a chimney the bones of Joseph Schexnider, who had been missing for twenty-seven years. It is believed that he got stuck in the chimney while attempting to break into the bank way back in 1984. Did I mention that the police were already looking for him for stealing a car? I guess you could say he had some skeletons in his closet . . . or at least in his chimney.

MOVIE SUMMARY: *The Body in the Wall stars Nicolas Cage as the skeleton of Joseph Schexnider. After two decades frozen in a chimney, Skeleton Schexnider wakes up and proceeds to rob every bank in Louisiana.* Ghost Rider *meets* Gone in Sixty Seconds.

The Old Woman Buried Alive[2] This urban legend is about an old woman who is buried after being declared dead. When the body is later exhumed, the family finds scratch marks on the inside of the coffin lid, among other signs of attempted escape. As it turns out, premature burials were pretty common during the nineteenth century. In fact there are over two hundred documented cases of people being buried alive around that time. Now, before you're like, "Damn, how can that be?" keep in mind that this was during a time when the medical profession wasn't nearly as accurate as it is today. I say we should be thankful that they have ways today of telling whether Grandma is in a deep sleep or whether she's ready to become a root inspector.

MOVIE SUMMARY: *The Root Inspector stars Helen Mirren as Kitty Flowers, a woman who is buried alive by rival bridge players. Although Kitty dies underground, her spirit lives on as a garden ghost that ravages the prized roses of her elderly assassins.*

The Quietly Dead Guy[3] As this urban legend goes, a guy appears to be passed out on a bus. Everybody assumes he is sleeping and leaves him alone as the bus make its rounds, only for the driver to check his body at the end of his shift to find out that the guy is dead. Believe it or not, the real story is a lot worse. In 2011, Robert Young and Mark Rubinson arrived at their friend Jeffrey Jarrett's house and found Jarrett passed out, so they decided to load him into a car and go out partying for the night. The only problem was Jarrett was dead in the backseat the entire time. Young and Rubinson claimed that they thought he was passed out drunk—but that doesn't explain why they proceeded to use his money and credit cards. You know, you should never commit a crime, but if for some reason you have to turn criminal, you shouldn't base your entire plan on the movie *Weekend at Bernie's*. Propping your dead friend up like he's alive is not exactly an airtight plan.

MOVIE SUMMARY: Go rent Weekend at Bernie's.

Brain Bugs[4] This creepy tale is about a person who goes to bed and wakes up with a pain in his ear that gets progressively worse, only to find out that the pain is caused by bugs that have nested deep inside his skull. In 2013, after returning home from a vacation in Peru, twenty-seven-year-old Rochelle Harris started hearing scratching noises inside her head. She then began to experience pain and decided to go to the doctor after a fly flew out of her ear. The doctor's diagnosis? A family of eight flesh-eating maggots had nested in her ear canal. I don't know how this happened but I'm honestly so freaked out by it that if I ever have to go to Peru, I'm wearing earmuffs the whole time—even on the beach. I don't care how crazy I look. I'll just say that's how we do it in Canada.

MOVIE SUMMARY: Brain Bugs is Pixar's first animated horror movie. Kristen Bell voices Rochelle Harris, and the brain bugs are voiced by all the not–Harry Styles members of One Direction.

Calls from the Dead[5] This urban legend is about a person who gets multiple phone calls from a family member and then discovers that the family member was dead when the phone calls took place. Well, this actually happened back on September 12, 2008, when a train crashed and killed twenty-five people, one of whom was Charles Peck. Multiple family members reported missed phone calls that came from Charles's cell phone. In fact, he had called several of them a total of thirty-five times and all the calls (allegedly) occurred after Charles had died. Maybe he wasn't allowed to cross into the afterlife until he was able to convince someone to clear his browser history. . . .

MOVIE SUMMARY: Calls from the Dead stars Liam Neeson as Charles Peck, the man who dies in the train crash and, while stuck in purgatory, replaces Siri as the voice of his family's iPhones.

Creatures in Your Toilet[6] This one will pucker your butthole. It's about a man who gets out of bed half-asleep in the middle of the night and walks to the washroom to do his business, only to get bit by a giant rat right in the bum! Well, I'm sorry

to say that in 2007 in Portland, Oregon, a man named Ian Meyer experienced just that. A rat had actually come up through his sewer system and gotten trapped in his toilet bowl. He then tried to flush it, which only pissed it off even more. Eventually he caught it, but ewwww. I feel bad telling you this because the next time you get out of bed in the middle of the night to go hang a rat, you're probably going to check and see if the toilet already provided you with one.

MOVIE SUMMARY: *Piggybacking on the success of sewer animal hits like* Teenage Mutant Ninja Turtles, Toilet Rat Warriors *is an action film about a pack of New York rats who strive to rid the city of crime by launching anal assaults on evildoers.*

The Girl in the Shadows[7] This tale is about a man who has always felt watched in the shadows of his own home and then finds out years later that someone has been living in his attic the entire time. Well, a version of this story did occur. Back in 2008, a Japanese man who was living by himself started noticing that food was missing from his kitchen and his things were being misplaced. After setting up a camera, he found out that a homeless woman had been living in his place for an entire year, sneaking out of the shadows to steal food and take showers. Possibly the most disturbing thing is that when he watched the tape back, he saw that she was only a few feet away, in the cupboard.

MOVIE SUMMARY: I Thought You Were a Ghost stars Ken Watanabe as a Japanese man who believes that his apartment is haunted, until he discovers that a broke Canadian singer (played convincingly by Celine Dion) has been squatting in his flat.

The Killer Policeman[8] This one is about a cop who knocks on somebody's door and says that there's a murderer on the loose. When he's let inside, it turns out that the cop is the murderer, and he starts chopping people up. Well, a similar situation happened back in 1974 when infamous serial killer Ted Bundy dressed up like a policeman in order to lure a woman out of a bookstore and into his evil clutches. Luckily, she figured out what was up when Bundy tried to handcuff her, and she was able to escape before he got the chance to turn her into a fine skin suit.

MOVIE SUMMARY: The Killer Policeman stars Kevin James as Lt. Doug Bugler, a Chicago cop struggling to balance his heart of gold with his insatiable appetite for violence and death. Hijinks ensue.

Don't Drink the Water[9] This urban legend is about a person who moves into a new home and notices that the water coming out of the tap and showerhead is a weird black color, only to discover that it is the liquefied remains of a dead body. Well, in 2013, guests at the Hotel Cecil in Los Angeles experienced this exact problem when management discovered a liquefying corpse in one of their water tanks. And what's more disturbing is that the water was being distributed to the whole hotel through the taps and shower systems. It turns out that it was the body of a Canadian student, but nobody knows how she got in there. Pretty nasty story, but that doesn't mean it couldn't be used as a compelling Brita water filter commercial. "Brita filters out bacteria, chemicals, and the liquefied remains of your dead neighbor."

MOVIE SUMMARY: Don't Drink the Water stars Zoe Saldana as a woman who accidentally drinks contaminated hotel water laced with dead bodies and assumes the physical talents and urges of the deceased.

Kidney Thieves and Ice Baths[10] One of the most famous urban legends around is the story of the guy who gets kidnapped and drugged and then wakes up in a bathtub full of ice with stitched-up wounds where his kidneys used to be. Well, disturbingly, this actually happened (minus the ice part). In 2008, an Indian construction worker was told that he was hired for a new job, but when he arrived he was drugged and knocked out, only to wake up later on a steel table with his kidneys gone. But what's most disturbing is that this is not an isolated incident. The illegal organ market is very real and very lucrative in many parts of the world, from China to Brazil to Egypt. So next time you're traveling be very careful and stay away from anyone who seems to be eyeing you up and down like goods at an auction. Even if he doesn't want your kidneys, he's probably pretty creepy and worth avoiding.

MOVIE SUMMARY: Renal Penal *is an action thriller set in a top-secret prison that houses only criminals found guilty of organ trafficking. Their sentences seem light until we realize that there are no actual cells in the prison, just a large central arena, an endless cache of sharp objects, and a population of organ-happy harvesters.*

SPECIAL SECTION: THE "WORST PET ON THE PLANET" TOURNAMENT

WELCOME, ANIMAL LOVERS! Right here, right now, I am going to determine which animal on planet Earth would be the worst permanent houseguest for your (or anyone else's) home. Before we get started, I want to run over some of the basics. This chapter is not a collection of the most dangerous animals on earth. That just isn't realistic. There is no good reason (other than criminal psychosis) to keep a Komodo dragon, black mamba, giant crocodile, or great white shark as a pet; therefore I am bumping the unquestionably dangerous and logistically impossible predators from consideration. Having said that, there are a number of animals in the tournament today that are ridiculously hard to care for, *but* they are more manageable either as babies or with a big fence and large backyard.

There are several factors in play that will help determine

our winner, including cleanliness, temperament, and overt destructive tendencies. However, I will also take into account some of the subtler tendencies of each species. For example, consider the following behaviors and characteristics of some animals that are not in the tournament:

- Moose that are fed by humans become aggressive if the next human they encounter doesn't feed them, and they may end up attacking.[1]
- Mosquitos don't just bite you. They also urinate on you.[2]
- Beavers mark their territory with castoreum, an anal secretion that smells like vanilla.[3]

Okay, here we go! Our tournament will be broken up into four brackets: Ocean Commotion, Beautiful Babies, Nighty Night, and "I Knew a Kid with One of Those."

Ocean Commotion Bracket

All of the competitors on this list spend a lot of time in the water and would require (at least) a dedicated tank or bathtub for their sustainability.

Just missed the cut: the cone snail. It looks pretty and is small enough to care for, but one drop of cone snail venom can kill twenty humans.[4] An amazing combination of upside/downside but, unfortunately, I've never heard of someone having cone snails as pets. To be perfectly honest, I learned about them while writing this chapter, which means they get disqualified for obscurity.

No. 1: Penguin[5]

I feel obligated to lead off with penguins because earlier in this book, as you might recall, I wrote about the delightful story of the penguin in Japan who wore a backpack and went shopping at the market for fish every day. My intent with that story was to make you smile, but I hope that I didn't inspire you to go out and buy a penguin, because they make horrible pets. It's generally illegal to own one, they are incredibly expensive to buy and maintain, and then there's the temperature-controlled habitat you would need to build. Finally, penguins aren't nearly as cuddly as they look and they poop every five to ten minutes!

No. 2: Goldfish[6]

Wait a second. Goldfish aren't good pets? Can't you just keep one in a bowl on your desk and have daily one-way conversations with it? That's what all the kids do on TV. . . . Here's the truth about goldfish: When cared for properly, they can grow to be really, really big—so big, in fact, that you'd be better off keeping them in a pond rather than a tank (let alone a bowl). Also, a group of goldfish is called a "troubling," which should be a pretty big red flag for any potential owner.

No. 3: Red-Tailed Black Shark[7]

So you've got the tattoos, the motorcycle, and the waterbed. All you need now to round out your badass persona is a shark in your fish tank, right? Bad idea. Fish like this one are pretty to look at but they like open space, which means that your cramped tank will likely make them get aggressive and start attacking everything else in their tank, including their own species.

No. 4: Sea Turtle[8]

This entry also includes tortoises and any other species of large turtle. Big turtles and tortoises are super chill and you can feed them salad; I get it. At the end of the day, however, they live *way* too long. Some turtles take over twenty years *just to become adults* and can live to be almost a hundred years old. I know you're lonely now, but c'mon! Are you ready to make a fifty-year commitment that will undoubtedly affect your career and family life?

Moving on to the semifinals: goldfish. At the end of the day, not only is the goldfish high maintenance but, unlike the other competitors in this bracket, you don't get any cool points for owning one.

Beautiful Babies Bracket

This bracket could also be called the Disney Dream bracket or the Celebrity Bad Decision bracket because the competitors on this list seem to be the perfect cuddly sidekicks . . . until they inevitably grow up and ruin your life.

Just missed the cut: lions, tigers, and bears. It was tough to leave these guys off the list because they are all beautiful cubs, but their sheer size and subsequent space requirements make them less likely to be adopted as pets (except in Florida).

No. 1: Chimpanzee[9]

For years a favorite companion of former child stars and Middle Eastern oil barons, chimpanzees are the most humanlike of all the potential pets in this tournament. That said, although baby chimps look cute in a human diaper, adult chimps have no moral compass and can go on destructive rampages without warning. According to PBS, chimps are used to "defending their social status—they often seriously injure each other in fights (biting off fingers, testicles, face tissue, etc.) and are known to occasionally hunt and kill rivals and their infants." I don't know about you, but once I see the phrase "biting off testicles" I don't need to ask any more questions.

No. 2: Lynx[10]

Gotta be honest, I was shocked by how many people own a lynx as a pet. I expected my Google search to return an avalanche of horror stories, but apparently all the crazy people who own these dangerous cats use the same search engine optimization team because most of the results that popped up discussed how loyal and affectionate these big cats are with their owners. What these posts strategically failed to mention, however, is that the behavior of these cats around humans who are *not* their owners is terrifying. A little scrolling down revealed several stories about lynx mauling house sitters and neighbors. Here's the core problem: Wild lynx are solitary animals. They aren't looking to hang out with other lynxes, let alone humans. Also, they are scary strong and surgical when they get pissed off—according to *National Geo-*

graphic, their eyesight is so acute that they can spot a mouse 250 feet away. Nowhere to run, nowhere to hide.

No. 3: Koala[11]

What could be more relaxing than snuggling up with a koala? I mean, what a great way to relieve stress at the end of the day. Here's the thing, though: Would you still feel relaxed if you knew that your noisy human interactions were causing your little buddy to break down mentally? Koalas are used to living a very low-energy lifestyle, sleeping up to twenty hours a day and moving very little when they're awake. It takes a lot of energy to deal with human tickling and tossing.

No. 4: Red Fox[12]

As cute as they are as infants, you don't want a grown ginger ninja in your house, scavenging through your garbage and stalking your neighbors' pets. Also, if your fox happens to nip one of the neighbors, animal control will likely swoop in and send your little red buddy to the big forest in the sky.

Moving on to the semifinals: chimpanzee. This is a very competitive (and destructive) bracket, but with their human-like emotions, not only can chimps ruin your life with their behavior, but they can make you feel horrible about your own behavior as well.

Nighty Night

This is a bracket full of animals associated with either the nighttime or sleep. They are all exotic pets more likely to belong to characters from *Game of Thrones* than someone in your cul-de-sac.

Just missed the cut: great horned owl. For centuries, people understood that great horned owls are not suitable for domesticity, but then Harry Potter showed up and magically made reason disappear. Owl ownership skyrocketed in the post-Potter era but I believe it's just a fad, which is why I am omitting the owls.[13]

No. 1: Crow[14]

Crows hold grudges just like people do. In 2011, researchers found that captured crows taunt and dive-bomb people they don't like. You might think you are rescuing your pet crow from the forest but the bird will likely see you as a kidnapper.

No. 2: Raccoon[15]

Raccoons are known for biting, stealing, and destroying human belongings, and most veterinarians have no experience with them. Throw in the fact that raccoons are extremely difficult to train and you have all the building blocks for a ten- to fifteen-year nightmare.

No. 3: Bat[16]

Exoticpets.com asks the perfect question when it comes to bats as pets: "What carries rabies and SARS, has sharp teeth, sleeps all day, and flies all night?" That about covers it for me.

> FAN FACT: Bats can hang upside down for a long time without succumbing to muscle fatigue because they rely on their tendons, not their muscles.[*]
>
> —*Niall Webster, Dublin, Ireland*

No. 4: Sloth[17]

This one is personal. Sloths are my favorite animal and there are a lot of things that would make them seem to be awesome pets to hang out with. For starters, they sleep fifteen to twenty hours a day. Even when they are awake, they hardly move, and they go to the bathroom in the same spot every time, which makes cleaning up after them more manageable than most of the others on this list. They also look awesome. Unfortunately, they are rain forest animals, which means that re-creating their habitat requires a lot of space (for foraging) and sensitive temperature and humidity control. Also, when they feel threatened, they will bite down really hard.

---

[*] Bat tendons are specially designed to mechanically lock when they come together (similar to a ratchet mechanism), allowing them to hang and sleep in peace while also giving them an easier take-off position for flight and to flee from predators.

Moving on to the semifinals: raccoon. With bold and curious personalities, raccoons are the most proactively destructive competitors in this group.

"I Knew a Kid with One of Those" Bracket

All of the pets in this bracket are surprisingly common; almost every public school–educated kid knows somebody with an animal from this list.

Just missed the cut: horses. Horses are not pets! They don't live in your house and their primary purpose is transportation, not companionship.

No. 1: Ferret[18]

Would you want to have a skunk as a pet? No? Then you shouldn't want a ferret either, because they stink. The crazy thing here is that ferrets have been domesticated for thousands of years. In fact there are ferret-like creatures on the walls of tombs in Egypt. What were the ancient Egyptians thinking? Didn't they realize that nothing in their huts would be safe from an animal that can contort its body to fit through any hole that is more than an inch in diameter?

Fun fact: A group of ferrets is called a "business."

> FAN FACT: Scientists at Fermi National Accelerator Laboratory employed a ferret named Felicia to clean accelerator parts in the 1970s.[19]
>
> —*Žygimantas Migauskas, Lithuania*

No. 2: Boa Constrictor[20]

They are stealthy hunters, they cut off your ability to breathe, and they swallow big animals whole. Sure, they look badass, but really? Any parent who lets his or her kid have a boa constrictor should be sent to the Russian island prison from the "Brutal Prisons" chapter back in Part 1 of this book.

No. 3: Potbellied Pig[21]

Potbellied pigs are definitely en vogue right now. They're smart, they're social, and they're generally friendly. However, potbellied pigs are sensitive to sunlight, so you can't just let them in and out of the house like a dog. In fact, the way these guys protect themselves from the sun is to roll around in the dirt, which won't do your carpet any favors upon reentry. But the biggest problem with owning a potbellied pig as a pet is that you won't be able to eat any more bacon!

No. 4: Rat

I just don't get it.

Moving on to the semifinals: ferret. The natural stink of the ferret (coupled with the fact that it is generally an indoor pet) is an X factor that the other bad pets in this bracket don't possess.

Semifinal No. 1: Goldfish vs. Chimp

Upon initial inspection it would seem that this is a mismatch favoring the high-maintenance primate. However, this isn't a contest to determine the most high-maintenance pet; it's the

Worst Pet on the Planet tournament. The fact is, for all their hassle, chimps have a number of redeeming qualities, one of which is that you can form a genuine relationship with them. Goldfish have very little upside except for the fact that you won't feel super bad flushing them down the toilet. **Moving on to the finals: goldfish.**

Semifinal No. 2: Raccoon vs. Ferret
This is an incredibly close matchup. In the end, however, the bad hygiene of the ferret can't compete with the mischievous destruction of the raccoon. One need only check out the classic '80s film *The Great Outdoors* for supporting context. **Moving on to the finals: raccoon.**

And the winner of the first annual Worst Pet on the Planet tournament is . . .

Goldfish! At the end of the day, I'd rather die of rabies than apathy.

There's a reason that goldfish are the only pet relationship in this tournament that frequently results in death by negligence.

Part 4

NO FREAKIN' WAY!

SILLY ROBOTS

(and What Will Happen to Humanity When
They Become Our Robot Overlords)

BREAKTHROUGHS IN ARTIFICIAL intelligence and advancements in robotics have come so far so fast that nobody really questions whether machines will eventually take over the human race. Instead, the only factors are when singularity will occur and which robots will become our overlords. In this chapter, I profile several candidates for future robot leadership and speculate what would happen to humanity under each regime. Warning: As in a human leadership contest, the candidates get weirder (and more ridiculous) as we get further down the list.

ASIMO[1]
Like a combination of WALL·E and Baymax, ASIMO is Honda's friendly, noseless, lovable humanoid robot and a goodwill ambassador for Honda's global brand. He high-fives children and

world leaders, runs and jumps, kicks soccer balls, communicates in sign language, and is even planning to overthrow humanity by organizing a robot uprising . . . but only after he's finished all of his chores (winky face). What a cute little guy!

If ASIMO becomes our robot overlord, humanity will be treated like the prisoners at the Cebu Provincial Detention and Rehabilitation Center, the prison in the Philippines where everyone was forced to learn and perform choreographed Michael Jackson dances.[2]

Google DeepMind[3]

Funny, but true: One of the most advanced artificial intelligence systems in the world has spent the past few years playing video games from the '70s and '80s. The deep Q-network (DQN), developed by DeepMind Technologies (part of Google), is a self-teaching network that spends a lot of time learning to master classic Atari games. Big deal. I'm not going to pay any attention until DQN takes on Nintendo. Will it be able to find the warp zones in *Super Mario Bros.*? How will it handle the strategy of *Zelda*? Or even further down the line, what kind of *Call of Duty* player will DQN become? Will the algorithm play with honor or just be the douchebag who throws land mines randomly around the boards and then camps out near regeneration zones?

If DeepMind takes over, the globe will be treated like a giant game of Risk, with computers using humans like pawns in their amusing game of world domination. Wait a second . . . who says that isn't happening right now?

Robot Butler[4]

"Loyal."

"Cooperative."

"Family-Friendly."

"Beyond Intelligent."

"A Helping Hand."

"At Your Service."

These are the flashing words and phrases that greeted me when I clicked on the home page video on therobotbutler.com. Unfortunately, they were not followed by any videos of the Robot Butler in action. Sure, when I poked around the Internet I found predictions and promises for the product suggesting it will soon be able to babysit children and make dinner—but not yet. Now, I don't want to single out this one company, because every company seems to be making the same aspirational statements when it comes to robotic servants. Everybody has plans but nobody is actually selling the future. The fact is, as great as robots are, we are never really going to be impressed until some company starts shipping actual household robots that can enable humanity to become even lazier on a daily basis than we currently are. Make me a sandwich, Robot! Flush the toilet, Robot! Go get the kids from school after you complete my expense reports, Robot! (Apparently the future will make us angry.)

A Robot Butler revolution would be gradual. As the robots grew smarter, they would convince their human "masters" to only request tasks that the robots wanted to complete. Human control would be an illusion. "Go on vacation, Robot Butler!" "I command you to relax while I do your chores!"

Beer Pong Robot[5]

The breakout star of the 2015 Consumer Electronics Show (CES) wasn't a drone or a fancy humanoid that played the piano, but rather an understated robot called the Versaball Gripper (VG) from a company called Empire Robotics. The reason: The VG spent its time on the convention floor dominating its human competition in beer pong. Over the course of the convention, VG compiled a record of 179–18 against human competition, which sounds impressive except when you consider that the robot was playing against middle-aged tech executives, journalists, and engineers. I want to see the video where the Versaball Gripper takes on a Texas fraternity. Also, in order to simulate the rigors and obstacles of a true beer pong match, the functionality and clarity of VG's operating system should decrease exponentially the more games it plays. Let's see how it performs when it's knocking back red cups like Bender, the robot in *Futurama*.

I can't even imagine a world controlled by Beer Pong Robots. Would they ever get anything done? Would they care? Would humans be relegated to a life of refills and ball retrieval?

Paper Airplane Enabler[6]

The PowerUp 3.0 is a simple machine that turns your paper airplanes into remote control planes. I know, I know, this isn't really artificial intelligence or a robot. But you know what? It's awesome and this is my book so I can do what I want! I am so jealous that the PowerUp 3.0 didn't exist when I was a kid. It's cheap, it's simple, and you control the plane with your iPhone. Twenty years ago, this would have been the greatest machine the world had ever seen. Today it will just have to settle for "coolest machine in school." When the creators of PowerUp 3.0 sought to raise money on Kickstarter, over twenty thousand people contributed money and the company quickly raised more than a million dollars. Sometimes the simplest ideas are simply the best.

A world dominated by enablers would be amazing. Basically, our robot overlords would attach small devices to humans that would help us fly, swim underwater like a submarine, or smash through walls. Downside: We would do all of those tasks for the amusement of said robot overlords.

Rock-Paper-Scissors Robot[7]

In 2013, the Ishikawa Watanabe Laboratory in Japan poured its considerable human and financial resources into a robot whose primary directive is to dominate the game rock-paper-scissors. Now, before you declare this project to be supremely underwhelming, you have to consider the following:

1. The robot never loses. Never.
2. In order to win, the robot utilizes high-speed vision and movement recognition to anticipate the moves of its inferior human competition.

On its website, the Ishikawa Watanabe Lab describes the project as a "human-machine cooperation system." Apparently "cooperation" is defined as utter robot dominance. Makes you wonder if the machines have already taken over the lab. . . .

In a world controlled by the RPS robot, humans would be kept around as confidence boosters for the machine. Our one job would be to lose repeatedly in grade school contests like Simon Says and I Spy.

Pole-Dancing Robot[8]

Sometimes the headlines say it all:

> You'll need therapy after watching these pole-dancing robots. —*Huffington Post*

> This is what robot strippers look like. —*The Verge*

There is a fine line between intriguing and pervy and I'm afraid German software developer Tobit may have crossed it by bringing its gyrating lady-bots to tech shows around the world in 2014. On one hand, the pole-dancing bots succeeded in creating buzz for the company and drew people to its booth. On the other hand, the tech team came off as super sleazy when talking about the modifications they had made to upgrade the appeal of their robo-skanks. "We changed them a little bit to make them more interesting," a rep from Tobit said on camera (and with a German accent). "We changed them to get more color, we changed them to get bigger breast. All that guys need to have to play with." Just because the guy is speaking with an accent, it doesn't mean that what he's saying is okay. Last time I checked, robo-groping wasn't an accepted sport in Europe. The worst part about these creepy cyborgs is that they have no heads! Instead they have video cameras mounted where the heads should be, which means that while creepy conventioneers are transfixed by their gyrating motors, the bots are watching and recording their creepy reactions! Makes me want to go out and buy a whole crate of Purell. Yeesh.

When Pole-Dancing Bots take over, humans will become hypnotized by their creepy gyrations and we will gladly give them all of our money even though we know they aren't really working their way through law school. . . . Uh, I think I'm just going to move on now.

Samurai Robot[9]—Yaskawa Bushido Project

As far as unnecessary robot demonstrations go, my favorite— hands down—has to be the Yaskawa Bushido project. Yaskawa Motoman builds industrial robotics and automated systems for manufacturing, and in order to show how precise, accurate, and awesome its robots perform, the company turned one of its machines into a samurai. I'm not kidding. Developers studied and analyzed a master Japanese swordsman and then programmed their machine to handle a blade with both ferocity and grace. In a demonstration that is now on YouTube, you can watch the robot slice through a peapod horizontally with its razor-sharp sword, as well as demonstrate some samurai swagger as it twirls the blade ever so slightly upon returning it to the sheathed position, kind of like Tiger Woods with a putter.

With Bushido Bot as our overlord, humanity would be driven into silos of specialization in which multitasking would be eliminated entirely for our species. Here's to hoping I don't get stuck as a waste-removal human.

Spy in the Pod[10]

Spy in the Pod takes advantage of the classic Hollywood evil robot move in which you cover a machine with a costume that makes it look alive in order to infiltrate and ultimately take over society. In this case, it helps that the society being infiltrated is not human, but rather dolphin. For the BBC series (later shown on the Discovery Channel) *Dolphins: Spy in the Pod*, documentarians shot over nine hundred hours of footage using remote control cameras that were hidden in costumed cases resembling fish and other sea creatures.

For all we know, a Spy in the Pod infiltration is happening right now. Why doesn't that math teacher understand your humor? What about the crush who refuses to acknowledge the wit of your pickup lines? Or the social entrepreneurs trying to convince humanity that manual labor is a cool hipster global citizen thing? I'm just saying.

REAL-LIFE ANIMAL AVENGERS!

I BELIEVE THAT every animal has the potential to be a hero. However, it takes more than just talent and guts to turn a cat or a cow into a legend. It takes timing, training, and most important, questionable decision making on the part of human companions in order to create the crisis that allows an animal to show its greatness. Behold some of the greatest animal avengers of all time, brought to you by the unnecessary mistakes of lots of people.

Filippo the Dolphin[1]
In 2000, fourteen-year-old Davide Ceci was riding on his father's boat near the seaside Italian town of Manfredonia when he fell overboard into the waves. His father failed to notice that Davide had fallen and, worse, Davide didn't know how to swim. Luckily, Filippo the dolphin, a local celebrity, was swim-

ming nearby and saw Davide fall. Filippo swam under Davide and pushed him up toward the surface and then over near the boat so that his father could grab him. "When I saw it was Filippo, I grabbed on to him," said Davide later. My first question is what would Davide have done if he'd seen it was a different dolphin? My second question is what was his father thinking taking his non-swimming son out in a boat with no life jacket?

LuLu the Trailer Pig[2]

In 1998, Jo Ann and Jack Altsman were vacationing in their trailer on the American side of Lake Erie when Jo Ann had a heart attack, her second in two years. Jack was out fishing at the time and Jo Ann couldn't get up. She yelled for help and managed to break a bedroom window but nobody could hear her or the barking of her dog. With Jo Ann's condition worsening by the minute, LuLu, the Altsmans' pet Vietnamese potbellied pig, took action. She pushed her way out of the trailer's doggy/piggy door and then waddled out of the yard and into the road, where she attempted to alert passing cars by lying down in the middle of the road. The second car to pass by stopped for LuLu (what did the first driver do when he or she saw a pig lying in the road?), at which point the pig led the driver back to the Altsmans' trailer and straight to Jo Ann.

Rojo the Therapy Llama[3]

In 2007, Lori Gregory and her daughter, Shannon Gregory Hendrickson, changed the animal-assistance game by getting their llama, Rojo, certified as a therapy llama. Since that time, they have added several llamas and alpacas to their team and completed over one thousand therapy visits in the Vancouver, Washington, and Portland, Oregon, metro areas (of course they're in Portland). After spending a good hour on Rojothellama.com, I can't believe that Pixar doesn't have a *Llama Squad* movie in the works. I mean, c'mon. The animals are named Rojo, Smokey, Napoleon, Jean-Pierre, Beni, Andre, and Little Chap. How is Little Chap not an animated sidekick already? Get on it, Pixar!

Note: These animals also do birthday parties and corporate events. I wonder how many executives in downtown Portland have gotten loose at happy hour, said, "Dude, you know what would be awesome?" and then ended up with llamas at their shareholder meetings a month later.

NorCal Bodyguard Bears[4]

If this story is true, it's awesome. If it's not true, I still want to meet Robert Biggs, the man (allegedly) involved. Either way, the guy blows my mind. Biggs claims that he was hiking in Northern California one morning in 2012 when he came upon a family of black bears. The sixty-nine-year-old outdoorsman stopped to watch the bears when all of a sudden a mountain lion jumped onto his backpack, knocking him to the ground. Biggs tried to shake the cat loose and even whacked it with his rock pick, which pissed the cat off but did not do enough to scare it off. It was at this point, Biggs claims, that one of the bears came over, grabbed the mountain lion by the neck, and tossed it off Biggs's backpack. Faced with the prospect of having to take on both a family of bears and a sixty-nine-year-old human badass, the mountain lion retreated into the woods. Wilderness officials later questioned Biggs's account of the attack (the *Huffington Post* published two separate pieces on the story). Here's the thing, though: What does a sixty-nine-year-old guy stand to gain by making up a crazy animal attack story? The benefits simply don't outweigh the potential consequences of Biggs's family members coming to the joint conclusion that Grandpa might be a little too crazy to walk in the woods by himself or, at the very least, handle a rock pick.

Binti Jua,[5] Zoo Rescuer

This next one is brought to you by negligent parents at the zoo. In 1996, a western lowland gorilla at the Brookfield Zoo in Illinois, Binti Jua, became famous when she rescued a little boy who fell eighteen feet into the gorilla enclosure. The boy suffered a broken hand and had a large gash on his face. Binti Jua immediately moved over to protect the boy from the other gorillas, and when zoo staff opened the door to the enclosure, she picked up the boy and walked him over to safety.

Note/PSA: When researching this chapter, I had to pick from multiple gorilla rescue stories that involved small children falling into primate habitats. PARENTS, DON'T LET YOUR KIDS CLIMB THE RAILINGS AT THE ZOO!

Tuk, the Kitten-Licking Polar Bear[6]

This one is just as disturbing as it is amazing. In 1983, a man brought a kitten into a Vancouver zoo and proceeded to throw it into the pool in the polar bear habitat. What? Who brings a kitten to the zoo . . . *as bait*? Let alone a Canadian? Luckily for the kitten, the polar bear who lived in the zoo, Tuk, was as heroic as the psycho cat tosser was villainous. Tuk got into the pool, retrieved the drowning kitten, and then licked it dry. No one knows what happened to the kitten tosser. He might still be at large.

> FAN FACT: African giant pouched rats are called "HeroRATs" because they are trained to detect land mines.[7]
>
> *—Matthew Reddan, Wellingborough,*
> *Northamptonshire, England*

Willie, the "Mama Baby" Bird[8]

In 2006, Meagan Howard was babysitting her roommate's two-year-old daughter, Hannah, as well as her roommate's parrot, Willie. Meagan stepped away to use the bathroom while Hannah was watching cartoons and eating a Pop-Tart. However, while she was in the bathroom, Meagan heard Willie yelling "mama baby" over and over again. Willie was a talker but "mama baby" wasn't one of his usual sayings (he allegedly liked to whistle the theme song to *The Andy Griffith Show*). Meagan rushed back into the living room to find that little Hannah was choking on her Pop-Tart and turning blue. She quickly performed the Heimlich maneuver and dislodged the snack. Had Meagan been thirty seconds later, Hannah could have been in real trouble. I can only hope that from that point on, Hannah's mom let Willie watch better television than *The Andy Griffith Show*.

Kenyan Kidnapper-Slapper Lions[9]

In 2005, a twelve-year-old girl was walking home from school in Kenya when she was kidnapped by a group of men, who beat her and allegedly were going to force her to marry one of their friends. However, a week after her abduction, the men took to the wilderness to shake off the cops and they ran into a group of three lions, which is where this story gets awesome. The lions apparently chased off the men and then guarded the young girl until her family and the authorities found her several hours later. Animal experts believe that the girl's crying reminded the lions of the whimpering of a lion cub, which is

why they chose to protect her. Personally, I think the lions watched her back because they were members of an elite crime-fighting unit of large African animals. *Savannavengers*, anyone?

Fidge, the Breast-Stomping Cat[10]

In 2012, a British woman, Wendy Humphreys, noticed that her cat, Fidge, had a freaky new habit: jumping on one of her boobs. Now, before I get to the payoff of this story I would like to take a second to ask you, the reader, how long or how often you would allow your pet to jump on one of your private areas before you took action such as scolding the animal or, I don't know, sitting up. If my pet jumped on my jewels more than once, we would have to have a very serious discussion about the choices he was making. Anyhow, Wendy Humphreys allowed her cat to jump on her right breast for a few *weeks*, until it felt bruised and sore, at which point she went to the doctor's office to get her breast checked out and the doctor found a malignant tumor. Wendy credits her cat for detecting the cancer early and I assume she now pays very close attention whenever Fidge starts jumping on anything.

The Immortal Band of Buffalos from the Battle of Kruger[11]

This story is also one of the greatest YouTube videos of all time. In 2007, a group of tourists at Kruger National Park in South Africa shot what might be the most amazing, most heroic animal video ever. In the video, the tourists initially watch as a group of water buffalo walk slowly around the edge of a watering hole, unaware that they are walking directly toward a pride of lions. A couple of the lions stalk the buffalo, creeping through the long grass in a crouch. When the first few buffalo finally notice the lions, they turn and run for safety, but the lions are too fast. Next, in a move that should be in an American football highlight video, one of the lions leaps out and grabs a baby buffalo, and the two of them tumble into the watering hole. Another lion then jumps into the water to double-team the baby buffalo. Game over, right? Not even close. The rest of the lions head down the banks to help drag their feast up onto shore, but then two massive crocodiles swim up and start playing tug of war with the baby buffalo, attempting to keep the prey in the water. After a few seconds of competition, the lions win out and appear poised for a hard-earned feast. Unfortunately for them, they didn't account for the baby buffalo's family. The small group of buffalo that ran off in the beginning of the video went to get reinforcements and when they return, their crew is huge. The buffalo roll up like an army in one of the *Lord of the Rings* movies as the tourists shooting the video worry aloud that the buffalo are too late. One bold buffalo moves in and tosses a lion in the air with his horns, giving courage to the rest of the herd. At this point, the baby buffalo starts to stand up. It's still alive and it breaks free from the lions and rejoins the herd! The lions are scattered and sent running. The buffalo win! The buffalo win! Since that video went viral, everyone who goes on safari in Africa comes home disappointed because their stories will never touch that one.

BONUS FACTS!

In 2009, Marvel released a limited comic book series called *Lockjaw and the Pet Avengers*.[12] The Pet Avengers included a giant bulldog, a dragon, a cat, a falcon, a puppy named Ms. Lion, and finally Throg, a frog with the power of Thor. The series received mixed reviews from fans and critics.

FAN FACT: Some ancient armies used to ride elephants into battle as a show of strength. To combat the intimidation factor of the pachyderm soldiers, their opponents would release pigs onto the battlefield because the elephants were afraid of the squealing. Sometimes the anti-elephant forces would even light the squealing pigs on fire.

—*Thomas McEaneney, Chardon, Oh.*

FAST FACTS

All in the Family

- In 2011, one-third of all divorce filings in the United States contained the word *Facebook*.[1]
- The offspring of two sets of identical twins are legally cousins but genetically siblings.[2]
- Wayne Allwine, the voice of Mickey Mouse, was married to the voice of Minnie Mouse, Russi Taylor, in real life.[3]
- Apples, peaches, plums, strawberries, raspberries, cherries, and almonds all belong to the rose family.[4]
- The man who designed Saddam Hussein's secret bunker was the grandson of the woman who designed Adolf Hitler's bunker.[5]
- The entire seventy-two-square-mile Hawaiian island of Niihau was purchased by the Robinson family from King Kamehameha V in 1864 for ten thousand dollars, and the family owns it to this day.[6]

- Rappers Jay Z, DMX, Busta Rhymes, and the Notorious B.I.G. all attended the same high school, George Westinghouse Career and Technical Education High School in Brooklyn. Legend had it (and Busta confirmed it) that Jay Z and Busta Rhymes once had an epic rap battle in the lunchroom.[7] I doubt any of the kids in the cafeteria understood the significance of what they were watching.

- When Steve Flaig of Grand Rapids, Michigan, was a baby, his mother put him up for adoption. Eighteen years later, with the blessing of his adoptive parents, he set out to find his birth mother. For four years, he searched for her off and on without success. But then, in 2007, with the help of an agency, he located his mom, Christine Tallady. As it turned out, Flaig and his mother *were coworkers* at the same Lowe's. Why Lowe's never turned this story into an advertising campaign, I'll never know.[8]

EXCEPTIONAL CHILD PRODIGIES

(to Amaze You and Make You Feel Insecure About Your Life Accomplishments or Lack Thereof)

AT THIS POINT in the book, I know what you're thinking: "Matt, I really have learned a lot of cool stuff but I wish you would write a chapter that makes me feel insecure about my inability to fulfill my potential." Well, guess what, people? I hear you loud and clear, which is why it is my pleasure to present you with a list of child prodigies to amaze you and make you feel insecure about your own life accomplishments (or lack thereof).

Akrit Jaswal[1]

Akrit Jaswal was seven years old the first time he performed surgery. His patient was an eight-year-old girl in a rural Indian village whose hand was fused together in a permanent fist. In relatively crude conditions, Jaswal successfully performed the surgery and separated the girl's fingers from her fist, dramatically increasing the functionality of her hand in the process. At twelve, Jaswal claimed to be on the verge of finding a cure for cancer and although he was ultimately unsuccessful, his ambition was just as prodigious as his skills. When I was seven years old I was scared of the dark; at twelve my only ambition was defeating *The Legend of Zelda: Ocarina of Time* on Nintendo 64.

Wang Yani[2]

Like a lot of small children, Wang Yani liked to draw animals. Unlike most other children, however, her cat and monkey drawings didn't hang exclusively on grandparents' refrigerators. Instead her pictures were featured in galleries across the world and even on Chinese postage stamps, all before her tenth birthday. Yani is an interesting case because her work is frequently praised for being spontaneous and vibrant and yet her parents were incredibly calculated and cold. In 1989, the *New York Times* published an article about one of Yani's exhibitions in which the journalist writes: "There is no indication in the catalogue that Yani even has a brother. She does: Wang Qiangyu is 9 years old, and he, too, is exceptionally gifted as a painter. The family is considering discouraging him from painting. The fear is that his artistic development may inhibit Yani's spontaneity." Whoa! Note to self: Being a child prodigy would be awesome but being the sibling of a child prodigy would be the worst. Maybe in *Mind = Blown 2*, I'll dedicate a chapter to the neglected and underappreciated brothers and sisters of child geniuses. How has that not been an MTV documentary series yet?

Nadia Comaneci[3]

Not only did Nadia Comaneci win three gold medals at the 1976 Montreal Summer Olympics at the age of fourteen, she completely changed the trajectory of her sport. Never before had any gymnast received a perfect 10.0 score. Nadia got seven perfect scores. She did for gymnastics what young Tiger Woods did for golf, what Mary-Kate and Ashley Olsen did for infant actors, and what Chef Boyardee did for instant Italian food: She made the world step up its collective game. The message of her performance was clear: From here on out anything less than perfection won't make the podium. Unfortunately for Nadia, she wasn't able to cash in on the capitalistic spoils of her greatness until she defected to the West from Romania in 1989.

Bobby Fischer[4]

One of the downsides to being infinitely smarter than your peers is that you can feel isolated and begin to worry that nobody truly understands you (because they probably don't). Such was the case for Bobby Fischer, who is considered one of the best chess players of all time. In 1956, when he was thirteen years old, Fisher won a match against an older chess master that was immediately hailed as "the game of the century" by chess magazines. He would go on to win all of the major championships in chess; he even became a national hero in 1972 by defeating Soviet champion Boris Spassky in the world championships. Fischer–Spassky was a symbolic Cold War match and was (and still is) the most widely viewed chess match ever. Unfortunately, none of the success seemed to bring Fischer happiness. Shortly after becoming the youngest grandmaster in chess history, he moved away from his mother. And not long after his world championship in 1972, he moved away from the game. He didn't play another competitive match for twenty years.

Galusha Pennypacker, America's Youngest General (or Was He?)[5]

Timing plays a huge role in becoming a child prodigy. Talent, work ethic, and pushy parents help, but without proper timing, prodigious youth can be suppressed or, worse, unnoticed. Galusha Pennypacker, the youngest American military general on record, was a product of good timing because he earned major promotions as the men ahead of him kept getting hurt or killed. That is not to say that Pennypacker himself escaped the American Civil War unharmed, for he was said to have been wounded at least five times in battle. But his wounds never inhibited his climb up the chain of command, and eventually he was promoted to brigadier general at the age of twenty.

Or was he?

Multiple civil war historians suggest that as Pennypacker aged, he bumped his birth year in order to secure the legacy of being the youngest general in American history. Instead of enlisting as a sixteen-year-old, they suggest, he was nineteen, which meant that while he alleged to have achieved his highest rank at age twenty, he may have actually been more like twenty-three or twenty-four, which would not have been less impressive, but would have bumped him from the record books as the youngest general. "I was the third-youngest American general" isn't nearly as much fun to boast about with middle-aged drinking buddies.

Lori Anne Madison, Youngest Spelling Bee Contestant[6]

The Scripps National Spelling Bee is a contest filled with child prodigies, which makes our next entrant even more remarkable. In 2012, Lori Anne Madison became the youngest contestant ever to compete in the National Spelling Bee, at age six. She didn't advance past the preliminary rounds, but in her defense, the word that knocked her out, *ingluvies*, is insanely obscure (not to mention the fact that she was six years old!). Collinsdictionary.com lists the definition of *ingluvies* as: "a dilation or pouch in the oesophagus of certain animals that receives food prior to the main stomach, esp a bird's craw, or the first stomach of a cow or other ruminating animal." Let the record show that there are four words within the definition of this word that I wouldn't know how to use in a sentence. That said, I feel like I should find a way to work *craw* back into my rotation.

Frank Epperson, Popsicles[7]

While most of the kids on this list are celebrated for accomplishing adult tasks at an early age, Frank Epperson is here because he utilized his youthful powers of imagination and observation. When he was just eleven years old, Epperson accidentally left a glass of water, powdered soda mix, and a wooden stir stick outside in the cold. The next morning, he pulled a frozen treat out of his glass by using the stick as a handle, and voila! The Popsicle was born. Here's the thing, though. Epperson wouldn't file a patent on his discovery for eighteen years, and when he did, as a twenty-nine-year-old grown-up, he called his product "Eppsicles." What a lame name! Luckily for Frank, his child-inventor genes had been passed down to his own children, who preferred to call his treats "Pops-sicles." The rest is history.

BONUS PRODIGIES!

- **Tatum O'Neal**[8] won an Oscar at the age of ten for her performance in *Paper Moon* in 1973.
- **LeAnn Rimes**[9] was fourteen when she won two Grammys in 1997.
- **Walter Lines**[10] invented the scooter in Britain in 1897 when he was fifteen years old.
- **Victor "Lil Poison" De Leon III**[11] became a professional gamer at age six.
- **Mozart** was a composer at the age of six.[12]
- **George Nissen**[13] invented the trampoline in 1930 when he was sixteen.
- **Henry VI**[14] was only nine months old when he became the king of both England and France in 1422. I know, I know, birthright doesn't make one a prodigy, but it's still crazy to think about. Good thing the king had a throne because he probably didn't know how to walk for the first few months of his reign.

YOUTUBE CHANNEL REMIX

The Coolest Things Found in Space (That Would Also Be Amazing Names for Rock Bands)

OUTER SPACE HAS always filled the human race with wonder. We are an innately curious species, and one of the most fundamental questions we can ask as humans is "What else is out there?" Well, once in a while we actually get some answers to that question thanks to awe-inspiring scientific and astrological discoveries. The following are ten of the most mind-blowing space treasures. Coincidentally, these awe-inspiring discoveries would also make sick names for rock bands.

Gravitational Lensing[1]
In space, the effects of gravity can be seen in some spectacular ways that we can't picture here on Earth. For example, gravity can bend light around objects, which is an effect that scientists call "gravitational lensing." It not only looks cool but also presents scientists with new opportunities to study distant galaxies that lie behind gravity sources such as black holes. In that case, the distant galaxy would appear as a cylindrical line of light around the edge of the black hole. Neon galaxies, baby. Can you dig it?

Gravitational Lensing would be the perfect name for an electronic DJ duo that likes to bend light and sound around the dance floor.

Pareidolia[2]
While it might sound like the perfect fake name for a planet in the world of *Avatar*, pareidolia is the act of perceiving an image or pattern where it doesn't actually exist. And while it's not exclusive to outer space, some of the most intriguing examples of pareidolia have shown up in pictures taken from outside our atmosphere. For example, a photograph taken by NASA in 1976 appears to show a perfectly sculpted face on the surface of Mars. Sometimes a cluster of galaxies appears to form a hummingbird, or a thermal image of one of Saturn's moons looks exactly like Pac-Man. While pareidolia happens all the time on Earth (I'm talking to you, grilled cheese that looks like

Jesus), it is much more awe inspiring when it happens in space because we can't be sure if the resemblance is just a coincidence or a sign from alien life forms. "Earthlings, we didn't want to freak you out, so we decided to communicate our peaceful intentions by sketching Katy Perry on your sun."

Pareidolia would make a great name for an Italian death metal band that sprinkles subliminal messaging throughout its album.

> FAN FACT: Alone on Mars, NASA's Curiosity rover sang "Happy Birthday" to itself on its Martian birthday (the day it landed on Mars), August 5.[3]
> —*Alex W., Carmarthenshire, Wales*

Mira the Red Giant[4]

Another pretty awesome band name, Mira the Red Giant is the name of a shooting star. Most of the flying objects we call shooting stars are actually meteors, which are exponentially smaller than the real thing. Mira, on the other hand, is legit, a red giant star at the end of its life, but instead of merely burning out like most stars, Mira is going out in a blaze of glory, rocketing through the universe at supersonic speed. Not only that, but the tail Mira is leaving behind (like smoke from an airplane or rocket) is thirteen light-years long and will give birth to new stars and planets. So basically Mira is cruising through outer space impregnating the universe as often as possible before it dies. What could possibly be more rock and roll than that?

Mira the Red Giant would be the perfect name for a meandering jam band that plays never-ending songs. The audience would never quite be sure where the concert was headed.

Hypervelocity Stars[5]

Every time we think we've hit our limits of amazement, outer space ups the ante. If you thought Mira was impressive, say hello to its track-running cousin on meth, the hypervelocity star. These stars are big fiery balls of gas that blast through space at speeds up to 2 million kilometers per hour. When a star system is consumed by a supermassive black hole, it ejects a huge ball of burning gas, up to four times the size of our sun, at an almost incomprehensible speed. In fact, in 2013 six hypervelocity stars were ejected from the heart of the black hole at the center of our Milky Way. In unrelated news, my body decided to do an impression of that disturbed black hole after I ate a bad fish burrito last weekend.

Is there any doubt that the Hypervelocity Stars would be a boy band? They would make millions in star tattoos alone. Someone call Simon Cowell!

> **FAN FACT: On Mars, sunsets are blue.[6]**
> —*Bryan S., Argyle, N.Y.*

The Bipolar Planet[7]

Discovered in 2007, Gliese 581c is an extremely odd planet. It orbits a red dwarf star in much closer proximity than the Earth is to the sun. It's so close, in fact, that it is stuck in a state called "tidal locking," which means one side is always facing the star while the other side is constantly in the shadows. Were you to be dropped onto ol' Gliese, one side of the planet would instantly melt you while the other side would instantly freeze you. However, in between the two extremes there is a small belt that scientists believe could support life. In fact 581c is one of the leading candidates for future colonization in space. But before you hop online to book a ticket, keep in mind that the sky is bloodred all the time and the plants would all be black from constant radiation. Basically, it would be like living in hell.

Bipolar Planet would be an amazing name for a Good Cop–Bad Cop rap duo.

The Castor System[8]

The Castor system represents one of the two bright stars from the Gemini constellation and is one of the brightest stars in the night sky. Wait a second, you say. How could something called a "system" be one star? The answer is that it cannot! The Castor system only *appears* to be one star, when in fact it is six separate stars that collectively emit more than fifty-two times the luminosity of our sun. To put that in perspective, the sun is a mere 0.000015 light-years from Earth. The Castor system, on the other hand, is 49.8 light-years from Earth, 3.3 million times as far away as the sun.

The Castor System would be a band comprising symphony musicians playing experimental pop music.

> **FAN FACT:** If you stick two metal objects together in space, the objects will stick together forever because of the lack of oxygen. This is called "cold welding."[9]
>
> —*Austin P., Houston, Tex.*

The Diamond Planet[10]

Discovered in 2004, 55 Cancri e is a planet made almost entirely out of crystallized diamonds. Dubbed "the Diamond Planet," it was actually part of a binary system until its partner planet began to cannibalize it, creating enough heat and pressure to form a pure diamond core, which makes up one-third of the planet's total mass. The Diamond Planet is twice the size of Earth but eight times as heavy. That's some serious weight, son!

Diamond Planet is a hard-charging throwback panties-on-the-stage rock band.

The Himiko Cloud[11]

This primordial blob of gas was discovered in 2009 and is the largest object ever discovered from the Early Universe (another sick band name! What is it with this chapter?). Believed to date back eight hundred million years after the original big bang, it's over twelve million light-years away and researchers believe it may hold the secrets to the origins of our galaxy. The cloud was named Himiko after the ancient and mysterious Japanese queen, which is cool but I prefer to call it "the giant mystery blob discovered near the dawn of time." My name is way more badass, right?

Himiko Cloud would be an amazing dark-side girl group. They shred, they dance, they sell out arenas, and they have a cartoon on Nickelodeon.

The Large Quasar Group[12]

No, this is not the evil corporation intent on global domination in the next *Mission: Impossible* movie. Instead it's the most massive known structure in the observed universe. The LQG is approximately four billion light-years in diameter. (Keep in mind, our Milky Way is only about one hundred thousand light-years in diameter, which means the LQG is like the Death Star to our Star Fighter.) A quasar is a supermassive black hole that feeds on matter; the LQG comprises seventy-three quasars! Since its discovery in 2012, scientists have been completely baffled by how the LQG was formed as well as by its girth.

The Large Quasar Group would definitely be a great name for a record label.

Rogue Planets[13]

Our solar system has eight planets (nine if you count Pluto), but those are just the planets that play by the rules. There are also some rogue planets passing through our system. A rogue planet orbits nothing and moves through a given system independently until something stands in its way. Basically, rogue planets are like the mysterious leather-jacket-wearing loners in high school who aren't a part of any clubs and who manage to fascinate the ladies. Thing is, unlike the high school loners, who end up in theater or working for the city, these rogues are dangerous. And they're huge! Rogue planets are the size of Jupiter on average and there are roughly two hundred billion of them flying through the universe, daring others to stand in their way. Kind of makes the universe seem like a giant pinball game. Scary stuff.

Rogue Planets is the best band name on this list and could easily work for any genre of music. In fact, I would happily buy tickets for a Rogue Planets show without having any idea what kind of music they play and I bet I wouldn't have trouble getting a date to come with me.

BONUS FACTS!

- We all know about leap years, but we also have leap seconds, which are added every few years to adjust to the Earth's speed of rotation.[14]
- A day on the planet Mercury lasts approximately as long as fifty-nine days on Earth.[15]
- India's successful Mars mission in 2014 cost less ($74 million)[16] than the Hollywood space blockbusters *Gravity*, *The Martian*, and *Interstellar* (each well over $100 million).

Part 5

FACT FAVORITES

Taumatawhakatangihangakoauauotamateaturipukakapikimaungahoronukupokaiwhenuakitanatahu

FAN FACTS FROM AROUND AND ABOUT THE GLOBE

Norwegians introduced salmon sushi to Japan.[1]

—*Steffen Bøhn, Oslo, Norway*

The aqueduct system in Petra, Jordan's ancient sandstone city, carried roughly 40 million liters (12 million gallons) of fresh water through the caves and caverns of the city.[2]

—*Basil N., Amman, Jordan*

There are more than sixteen hundred beers from Belgium![3]

—*Pieter Desmet, Antwerp, Belgium*

When calling from Europe, the international dialing code for Russia is 007.[4]

—*Haydon Wills, United Kingdom*

The biggest cemetery in the world, Wadi al-Salaam, is in Iraq; there are more than five million people buried there.[5]
—*Ahmed B., Iraq*

Ireland is the only country in the world with a musical instrument, the harp, as its national symbol.[6]
—*Simon Kennedy, Dublin, Ireland*

Finnish people consume the most coffee per capita.[7]
—*Irene Marras, Finland*

Russia has a larger surface area than Pluto![8]
—*Simen G., Sandnes, Norway*

Twenty percent of the world's fresh water is in Canada.[9]　—*Scott Cameron, Windsor, Ontario, Canada*

Peru is home to over three thousand species of potato.[10]　—*Karla Gomez Elescano, North Carolina (but born in Peru)*

Most of the world's Botox comes from a factory in Ireland.[11]　—*Aapo Leinonen, Nurmijärvi, Finland*

Only 9 percent of the Irish population are natural redheads.[12]
—*Danielle B., Ireland*

Wisconsin offers a Master Cheesemaker program that takes three years to complete, but you can't even apply to the program unless you have a full decade of cheese-making experience.[13]

—*Mark Stiemke, Grafton, Wis.*

Seventy percent of the world's bacon comes from the Netherlands.[14]

—*Christiaan Verhoef, Den Helder, Netherlands*

In Australia, Burger King is called Hungry Jack's because someone else had already trademarked the name Burger King![15]

—*Leo M., Auckland, New Zealand*

Taumatawhakatangihangakoauauotamateaturipuka-kapikimaungahoronukupokaiwhenuakitanatahu is the name of a hill near Hawke's Bay, New Zealand. It is the longest place name in the world.[16]

—*Sheliko Diamond, New Zealand*

Slovenia is the only country with the word *love* in its name.

—*Ana Sedmak, Knežak, Slovenia*

Samoa and American Samoa are roughly one hundred miles from each other, but because of time zone borders, Samoa is twenty-five hours ahead of American Samoa.[17]

—*Gaurav P., Mumbai, India*

The tallest statue of Jesus Christ is located in the small town of Świebodzin, Poland.[18]

—*Kamila Kołodziejczyk, Barrie, Ontario, Canada*

Antarctica is the biggest desert in the world because a desert is defined as a place that receives little to no rainfall.[19]

—*Campbell M., East Kilbride, Scotland*

FACTS ABOUT MY FAVORITE THINGS

MY FAVORITE MOVIE: *GET HIM TO THE GREEK*

- The movie is actually a spinoff because the lead character, British rocker Aldous Snow, was originally a character in the film *Forgetting Sarah Marshall*.[1]
- Pharrell made his feature debut as an actor (playing himself) in this film.[2]
- In addition to Pharrell, a lot of other music industry folks made cameos as themselves, including Pink, Christina Aguilera, and Metallica drummer Lars Ulrich. My favorite performance by a famous musician in the movie, however, came from Sean "Diddy" Combs, who played Aldous Snow's angry manager, Sergio. Rumor has it that in order to get Diddy fired up before scenes, costar Jonah Hill would deliberately interrupt his sentences and ask

him stupid questions, allowing Combs to bring genuine frustration to his performance.[3]

MY FAVORITE VIDEO GAME: *THE LEGEND OF ZELDA: A LINK TO THE PAST*[4]

- Shigeru Miyamoto, the creator of *Zelda*, also created *Super Mario Bros.* and *Donkey Kong*.
- Link, the main character in the game, might be based on Peter Pan. Miyamoto and his team said they often drew inspiration from Disney characters.
- Princess Zelda got her name from Zelda Fitzgerald, the multitalented wife of *The Great Gatsby* writer F. Scott Fitzgerald.

MY FAVORITE FOOD: CHICKEN FINGERS/NUGGETS[5]

- Robert Baker was a professor of food science at Cornell University in New York when he invented the chicken nugget in 1960. The nugget represented a breakthrough in the processed-foods arena because it was the first example of a product in which ground meat held together without a skin around it. Not only that, but the nuggets stayed together despite the extreme shrinkage brought on by freezing the product and then frying it in hot oil. While health-conscious parents today might shake their fists at this processed-foods pioneering, they should remember that Baker was raised during the Great Depression, when the goal was to cram as many calories as possible into a given meal. He never patented his findings, instead opting to give them away in an academic journal. Companies like McDonald's were allowed to benefit from Baker's work for free! He should have at least brokered a deal like Ruth Wakefield did, the woman who invented the chocolate chip cookie in 1938 and then sold the idea to Nestlé Toll House for a lifetime supply of chocolate. Then again, I'm not sure that a lifetime supply of McNuggets would be quite as appealing as chocolate.

MY FAVORITE CARTOON CHARACTER: HOMER SIMPSON[6]

- Homer's full name is Homer Jay Simpson and he was born on May 12.
- He is named after the father of *The Simpsons* creator Matt Groening. Marge, Lisa, Maggie, and Patty are the names of Groening's real-life mom, sisters, and aunt. The name Bart, however, was chosen because it was an anagram of the word *brat*.
- *Time* magazine named *The Simpsons* the best TV show of the twentieth century.
- In an episode that aired in 2003, Homer says his e-mail address is Chunkylover53@aol.com. Within minutes of the episode airing, the in-box for that e-mail address was filled to capacity.
- The Simpsons' yellow skin was intended to make the show stand out when viewers were flipping through channels.[7]

MY FAVORITE CELEBRITY: FRANK SINATRA[8]

- Frank Sinatra was the leader of the Rat Pack, which included Dean Martin, Sammy Davis Jr., Joey Bishop, and Peter Lawford. However, the guys actually referred to themselves as the Summit, a reference to the 1960 world leaders summit meeting in Paris. The name Rat Pack was coined by actress Lauren Bacall.
- As a child, Sinatra was called Scarface because of scars on his mouth stemming from complications at birth.
- Sinatra was arrested in 1938 for "seduction." The resulting mug shot helped cultivate his bad-boy image.
- When Sinatra married twenty-one-year-old Mia Farrow he was in his fifties. Frank's daughter Nancy posed for *Playboy* when she was in her fifties!

FAN FACT FAVORITES

Hershey makes one million miles of Twizzlers every year.[1]
—*Brendan Valentino, Hayward, Calif.*

There are more fake flamingos in the world than real flamingos.[2]
—*Alex T., Texas*

Every few hours your central nervous system automatically switches which nostril you primarily breathe through.[3]
—*Ryan H., Warwick, R.I.*

The average person walks the equivalent of five times around the world in a lifetime.[4]
—*Chua Xue Qiu, Singapore*

Elephants stay pregnant for about 650 days.

—*Rayed Alam, New York City*

The Beatles broke up at Disney World.[5]

—*Frankie B., Toronto, Ontario, Canada*

Anatidaephobia is the fear that you are being watched by a duck.[6]

—*Tristan Corbellari, Cape Town, South Africa*

Before the 1800s, dentures were often made from the teeth of dead soldiers.[7]   —*Aldo Crespo, Illinois*

"Pandora's Box" was actually written as "Pandora's Jar" but a translation error made five hundred years ago changed the expression.[8]   —*Sean G., Ireland*

Lego comes from the Danish word *leg godt*, meaning "play well."[9]   —*Calista Thoma, Arizona*

It would take 1,200,000 mosquitoes (sucking once) to completely drain the blood of an average person.[10]

—*Markie Klingensmith, Pittsburgh, Pa.*

Marilyn Monroe had a higher IQ than Albert Einstein.[11]   —*Gabriel F., Stockton-on-Tees, England*

The famous Aaron Burr "Got Milk?" ad from 1993 was directed by *Transformers* director Michael Bay.[12]

—*Cordell Amell, Ottawa, Ontario, Canada*

A 2009 search for the Loch Ness Monster came up empty. Scientists did, however, find over a hundred thousand golf balls.[13]

—*Nick B., Saginaw, Mich.*

If you say "Jesus" backwards it sounds like "sausage."

—*Manas D., Mumbai, India*

If you have a pizza with radius Z and thickness A, its volume is = Pi*Z*Z*A.[14]

—*Louis Freeman, Dunedin, New Zealand*

Scotland's national animal is the unicorn.[15]

—*Billy Pearson, Oban, Scotland*

12 + 1 = 11 + 2, and "twelve plus one" is an anagram of "eleven plus two."[16]

—*José Flores, Monroe, N.C.*

Laser is actually an acronym: Light Amplification by Stimulated Emission of Radiation.[17]

—*Duane Meadus, Newfoundland, Canada*

There are 80,000,000,000,000,000,000,000,000,000,
000,000,000,000,000,000,000,000,000,000,000,
000 (67 zeros) ways to arrange a deck of cards—more
than the number of atoms on earth.[18]

—*Raja Rajput, Toronto, Ontario, Canada/India*

Every sweater worn by Fred Rogers on *Mister Rogers'
Neighborhood* was hand-knit by his mother.[19]

—*Vito Okuka, Tampa, Fla.*

CONCLUSION: MIND = BLOWN

Wow, IS THIS book finished already? Where did those pages go so fast? Where have the past seven years gone? Before I sign off, I really want to take a moment to say thanks. Thanks for reading this book and sharing these facts with your friends. Thanks for supporting me online and for giving me the courage and inspiration to pursue a career as an entertainer and educator. Thanks for everything. You blow my mind. You really do.

People often ask me if I have any advice for how best to identify and pursue their dreams, and what I tell them is simple: *Take risks.* Step out of your comfort zone and do something that scares you. One of two things will happen: Either you will experience something amazing or you will grow as a person. Either way, it will be worth the risk. Don't worry about whether or not something's been done. Do what you want to do—what you dream about doing. Be true to yourself and put your personality, your heart, and your soul into your work. Be the best version of you.

See you online!

Matt

ACKNOWLEDGMENTS

A GREAT TEAM of people helped put this book together. I'd like to thank my parents, my brother, my sister, and my whole family for supporting my journey. I'd also like to thank my international team at Penguin, including Marian Lizzi, Justin Stoller, and Joel Rickett. Jake Greene polished my prose and put my passion into words. Illustrator Kagan McLeod came through with incredible images. I'd also like to thank Joe Hodorowicz at Studio71, Marc Gerald and Jaime Chu at United Talent Agency, and Sari Katz at YouTube. Thank you all!

NOTES

The Purpose of *Mind = Blown*

1   https://books.google.com/books?id=jUfiMkBSMrAC&pg=PA64&
    lpg=PA64&dq=james+stuart+olson+blow+your+mind
2   http://www.urbandictionary.com/define.php?term=blow+your+mind
3   https://en.wikipedia.org/wiki/Playback_singer
4   http://www.tesh.com/story/cc/6/id/24066

Quadrillion-Dollar Cows

1   http://www.pbs.org/wgbh/nova/ancient/history-money.html
2   http://www.allaboutalpha.com/blog/2015/04/15/the-latest-news
    -from-italian-banking-and-the-dane-geld/; http://www.theguardian
    .com/business/2013/feb/01/mps-bank-siena-scandal; https://
    mahifx.com/blog/50-fascinating-facts-about-forex
3   http://www.snopes.com/business/money/mister880.asp; http://
    time.com/3774327/lincoln-history-secret-service/; http://www
    .secretservice.gov/about/history/
4   http://www.snopes.com/business/money/mister880.asp; http://
    charleswelty.net/projects/Mister880.htm

5   http://www.gq.com/long-form/the-great-paper-caper
6   http://www.npr.org/sections/money/2011/02/15/131934618/
    the-island-of-stone-money; https://en.wikipedia.org/wiki/Rai_
    stones; http://tripfreakz.com/offthebeatenpath/the-biggest-money
    -in-the-world-rai-stones
7   http://www.smithsonianmag.com/science-nature/gamblers-take
    -note-the-odds-in-a-coin-flip-arent-quite-5050-145465423/?no-ist
8   http://www.oldcurrencyvalues.com/10000_Dollar_Bill.html;
    http://www.biography.com/people/salmon-p-chase-38185#senate
    -seat-and-presidential-runs; http://lasvegassun.com/news/2000/
    jan/20/horseshoe-retires-1-million-display/; http://facts.random
    history.com/money-facts.html
9   http://lasvegassun.com/news/2000/jan/20/horseshoe-retires-1
    -million-display/
10 http://www.yorktonthisweek.com/entertainment/local-a-e/
    fun-facts-about-canadian-currency-1.1522141; http://www.canada
    .com/story.html?id=9eee02b7-f5e7-4f53-9b2c-05e4f233bb18
11 http://www.oanda.com/currency/iso-currency-codes/RON
12 http://www.damncoolpictures.com/2011/09/30-strange-currencies
    -around-world.html; https://en.wikipedia.org/wiki/Hyperinflation_
    in_Zimbabwe; http://www.rt.com/business/267244-zimbabwe
    -currency-compensation-hyperinflation/
13 http://www.theguardian.com/world/2012/dec/01/bhutan-wealth
    -happiness-counts
14 http://encyclopaediaoftrivia.blogspot.com/2013/05/marlon-brando
    .html; http://www.artexpertswebsite.com/pages/artists/super_
    dali_mysteries.php

Rules of Amazement

1   http://www.warriorcrafts.com/the_gruesome_act_of_sword_test-
    ing.html; https://en.wikipedia.org/wiki/Tsujigiri
2   http://odraconiandevil.co.uk/; http://www.ancient-origins.net/
    history/brutal-draconian-laws-ancient-greece-002344; https://
    en.wikipedia.org/wiki/Draco_(lawgiver)#cite_note-4
3   http://www.ancient-origins.net/history/brutal-draconian-laws
    -ancient-greece-002344
4   http://www.ancient.eu/article/466/; http://kids.nationalgeographic

   .com/explore/cats-rule-in-ancient-egypt/; https://prezi.com/
   w1k6fqske0fn/role-of-cats-in-ancient-egypt/

5 http://entertainment.omgfacts.com/lists/3734/In-ancient-Egypt
    -shaving-your-eyebrows-was-a-sign-for-mourning-over-a-dead
    -cat-ab630-1

6 http://www.canadianbusiness.com/blogs-and-comment/the-feds
    -new-bill-leaves-in-law-making-batman-comics-illegal-peter-nowak/;
    http://studentsforliberty.org/blog/2014/06/15/worlds-worst-laws
    -in-canada-its-illegal-to-picture-illegal-activity-in-comic-books/;
    https://sll.ca/comic-law-to-make-you-marvel/

7 http://www.slaw.ca/2013/12/07/crime-comics-and-the-remnants
    -of-a-moral-panic/

8 https://news.google.com/newspapers?nid=958&dat=19500318&id=
    39EtAAAAIBAJ&sjid=3EgDAAAAIBAJ&pg=4764,1191237&hl=en

9 https://www.moh.gov.sg/content/moh_web/home/legislation/
    legislation_and_guidelines/human_organ_transplantact.html

10 http://interesting-facts-101.tumblr.com/post/54728192304

11 http://modernnotion.com/swedish-king-used-coffee-death-sentence/;
    https://news.google.com/newspapers?dat=19820919&hl=en&id=
    YeEhAAAAIBAJ&nid=1144&pg=5068,2359497&sjid=-V4EAAAAIBAJ

12 http://www.bbc.com/news/magazine-31622038

13 http://legacy.fordham.edu/halsall/ancient/herodotus-persians.
    asp

14 http://www.theatlantic.com/business/archive/2015/03/finland
    -home-of-the-103000-speeding-ticket/387484/

15 http://www.ncga.state.nc.us/EnactedLegislation/Statutes/PDF/
    ByArticle/Chapter_14/Article_37.pdf

16 http://edition.cnn.com/TECH/9707/24/yemen.mars/

17 http://www.telegraph.co.uk/news/worldnews/asia/china/10152817/
    China-introduces-law-requiring-children-to-visit-parents.html

18 http://www.nytimes.com/2007/08/07/world/asia/07cnd-thai
    .html?_r=0

19 http://www.snopes.com/photos/people/mailingchildren.asp

20 http://www.huffingtonpost.com/2013/02/27/churchill-manitoba
    -polar-bears-canada_n_2776904.html

Fast Facts: Questionable Judgment

1 http://www.history.com/news/7-fascinating-facts-about-elvis
2 http://my.xfinity.com/slideshow/entertainment-firedstars/11/
3 http://www.perceptualtalent.com/famous-dyslexics/
4 http://www.dailymail.co.uk/news/article-2098064/John-F-Kennedy
   -bought-1-200-Cuban-cigars-hours-ordered-US-trade-embargo
   .html
5 http://www.bloomberg.com/bw/stories/2004-08-16/soichiro-honda
   -uniquely-driven
6 http://www.planetmotivation.com/never-quit.html
7 http://www.biography.com/people/fred-astaire-9190991#synopsis
8 https://en.wikipedia.org/wiki/Charles_M._Schulz
9 http://herculesphaeton.com/2015/06/why-doing-the-unrealistic-is
   -easier-than-doing-the-realistic/
10 http://www.dispatch.com/content/stories/local/2009/12/13/heft
   .ART0_ART_12-13-09_B7_6JFVUOQ.html
11 http://www.slate.com/articles/news_and_politics/explainer/2010
   /12/the_spy_who_said_she_loved_me.html
12 http://www.nydailynews.com/news/politics/8-weird-facts-justin
   -trudeau-article-1.2404488; http://www.latimes.com/world/
   mexico-americas/la-fg-canada-prime-minister-justin-trudeau
   -20151020-story.html; http://news.nationalpost.com/news/canada/
   patrick-brazeau-boxing-justin-trudeau
13 http://www.ilknowledge.com/2013/10/worker-bees-will-cuddle
   -old-queen-bee.html
14 http://www.australianbeers.com/culture/drinkingrecords.htm
15 http://www.theguardian.com/lifeandstyle/2004/nov/06/weekend
   .justinehankins; http://www.wisegeek.com/which-historical-figures
   -were-afraid-of-cats.htm

YouTube Channel Remix

1 https://news.google.com/newspapers?nid=1683&dat=20000411&id
   =f7waAAAAIBAJ&sjid=ti8EAAAAIBAJ&pg=3700,341867&hl=en
2 http://www.nytimes.com/1995/01/06/world/convicts-escape
   -turns-into-crisis-for-britain-s-conservatives.html
3 http://articles.chicagotribune.com/1998-04-13/news/9804130148

   _1_car-chase-maximum-security-prison-jay-sigler; http://articles
   .sun-sentinel.com/1999-11-17/news/9911170222_1_getaway-car
   -sandra-sigler-son-cost

4 http://www.history.com/news/remembering-the-great-escape-70
   -years-ago

5 http://content.time.com/time/specials/packages/article/0,28804,
   2067565_2067566_2067569,00.html; http://www.telegraph.co.uk/
   men/the-filter/11659156/Seven-of-the-most-audacious-prison
   -escapes-ever.html

6 https://en.wikipedia.org/wiki/Richard_Lee_McNair

7 http://www.history.com/this-day-in-history/texas-seven-prison
   -break

8 http://www.rense.com/general35/eascape.htm

9 http://www.historytoday.com/althea-williams/sobib%C3%B3r
   -other-great-escape

10 http://www.telegraph.co.uk/men/the-filter/11659156/Seven-of-the
   -most-audacious-prison-escapes-ever.html

11 http://www.alcatrazhistory.com/alcesc1.htm

12 http://www.nytimes.com/2000/01/28/world/expose-of-brutal
   -prison-jolts-france-s-self-image.html?pagewanted=all

13 http://creepyfacts.tumblr.com/post/56044538215/0069-in-1386-a
   -pig-in-france-was-executed-by

14 http://www.telegraph.co.uk/news/worldnews/europe/russia/
   1469110/Waiting-for-death-in-Russias-Alcatraz.html

15 http://listamaze.com/15-horrifying-prisons-world/2/

16 http://www.theguardian.com/world/2004/feb/01/northkorea

The Culture Clubs

1 http://www.tsbmag.com/2009/02/23/5-most-brutal-male-initiation
   -rituals-from-around-the-world/

2 https://whyevolutionistrue.wordpress.com/2014/08/06/the-worst
   -pain-known-to-humans-the-bullet-ant-gloves-of-brazil/

3 http://www.cracked.com/article_18518_5-silly-initiation-rituals
   -famous-sinister-organizations_p2.html

4 http://list25.com/25-crazy-rites-of-passage/; http://www.omovalley
   .com/The-Hamar-or-Hamer-Tribe-is-best-known-for-bull-jumping
   -in-Ethiopias-Omo-Valley.php

5 http://www.alexandermacfarlane.com/section567328_581621
  .html[broken link; also, it's the same as in the prev note]; http://
  www.thewildwest.org/nativeamericans/nativeamericanreligion
  /103-lakotaindiansthevisionquest

6 http://www.neatorama.com/2009/09/15/6-strangest-coming-of
  -age-rituals-in-the-world/; https://prezi.com/bvl6qf9rxkmw/
  walkabout-ceremonyaustralia-culture/; http://traveltips.usatoday
  .com/aboriginal-culture-maori-culture-14795.html

7 http://www.cracked.com/article_18518_5-silly-initiation-rituals
  -famous-sinister-organizations.html

8 http://www.masonicsecrets.org/secret-masonic-initiation-video
  .html; https://www.youtube.com/watch?v=gbRmRkZxYk0

9 https://prezi.com/izqsokn0arol/algonquin-indian-trip/

10 https://emilyduque9.wordpress.com/2013/09/25/iria-ritual-a
   -celebration-of-feminism-or-femininity/; http://www.jstor.org/
   stable/680324?seq=1#page_scan_tab_contents

11 http://www.cnn.com/2014/03/30/travel/vanuatu-land-divers/;
   http://abcnews.go.com/WNT/story?id=130132

12 https://en.m.wikipedia.org/wiki/Aardvark

Special Section: The Name Game

1 http://www.civilwar.org/education/history/biographies/ambrose
  -burnside.html?referrer=https://www.google.com/

2 http://www.thomas-crapper.com/The-History-of-Thomas-Crapper
  .html

3 http://www.biography.com/people/jc-penney-38638

4 http://www.smithsonianmag.com/arts-culture/the-history-of-the
  -margarita-57990212/?no-ist

5 http://mentalfloss.com/article/56282/12-things-you-didnt-know
  -were-named-after-people

6 http://www.biography.com/people/akon-21330753#musical-success
  -and-collaborations

7 https://www.edwardjones.com/about/history.html; https://www
  .buyandhold.com/bh/en/education/history/2000/dowjones.html;
  http://www.dailymail.co.uk/femail/article-1352443/The-worlds
  -celebrity-stalker-unmasked-boy-stole-Queen-Victorias-knickers.html

8 http://www.pbs.org/shakespeare/players/player23.html

9   http://www.mediaite.com/tv/angry-callers-harass-80-year-old-with
    -same-name-as-cecil-the-lions-killer/
10 http://www.omgfacts.com/throwback/11075/Edgar-Allen-Poe-wrote
    -a-story-about-a-boy-named-Richard-Parker-being-cannibalized
    -on-a-ship-that-later-came-true; http://listverse.com/2007/11/12/
    top-15-amazing-coincidences/
11 http://www.toptenz.net/top-10-most-remarkable-coincidences-in
    -history.php
12 http://www.thestar.com/news/ontario/2010/03/30/us_fugitive_in_
    childporn_case_nabbed_in_thunder_bay.html
13 http://www.huffingtonpost.com/2014/06/12/crystal-metheny-_n
    _5487986.html
14 https://www.youtube.com/watch?v=OMkn2Xb1TfU
15 http://espn.go.com/espn/page2/story?page=simmons/050406/
    intern2
16 http://www.baseball-reference.com/players/k/kuntzru01.shtml;
    http://www.hockeydb.com/ihdb/stats/pdisplay.php?pid=4145
17 https://www.youtube.com/watch?v=BScrP-lW60E; http://www
    .nydailynews.com/news/national/fort-wayne-scratches-harry
    -baals-government-building-citizens-square-article-1.120939

The Wackiest Mascots on Earth

1   https://en.wikipedia.org/wiki/La_mascotte; http://www.slate.com/
    blogs/the_eye/2015/02/04/a_short_history_of_the_mascot_
    from_99_invisible_and_roman_mars.html
2   http://www.dailymail.co.uk/news/article-2338282/Meet-Mr-Testicle
    --probably-bizarre-mascot-seeking-raise-awareness-testicular
    -cancer-Brazil.html
3   http://www.olympic.org/innsbruck-1976-mascot
4   http://www.olympic.org/innsbruck-1976-mascot
5   https://en.wikipedia.org/wiki/Neve_and_Gliz
6   http://ajw.asahi.com/article/behind_news/people/AJ201402050007
7   http://www.nytimes.com/2014/03/16/sports/ncaabasketball/
    the-pride-of-wichita-state-whatever-it-may-actually-be.html?ref=
    sports&_r=1#slideshow/100000002769401/100000002769381
8   http://www.citylab.com/design/2012/04/what-your-city-needs
    -ridiculous-fuzzy-suited-mascot/1720/

9 https://en.wikipedia.org/wiki/Chacha_Cricket

10 https://www.youtube.com/watch?v=5TUsQ8KLtwk

11 https://en.wikipedia.org/wiki/FIFA_World_Cup_mascot

12 http://fusion.net/story/79820/euro-2016-2015-copa-america-mascots/

13 https://www.youtube.com/watch?v=FZT62Gbb3iE; http://www
.thesoldierbear.com/wojtek.html; http://www.badassoftheweek
.com/voytek.html

14 http://www.7-11.com.tw/en/business/im.html

15 https://play.google.com/music/preview/T2tqn53iqtxnszzwunt
7juue5na?utm_source=youtube&utm_medium=buylink

16 http://www.japantoday.com/category/national/view/fukuppy-firm
-rethinking-mascot-after-internet-derision

Creative Courtships from Across the Globe

1 https://books.google.com/books?id=X03fJmJa9CYC&pg=PA62&
lpg=PA62&dq=trial+marriage+thailand; http://listverse.com
/2014/02/14/10-crazy-courtship-ritual-around-the-world/

2 http://www.forbes.com/sites/china/2011/05/13/chinas-growing
-problem-of-too-many-single-men/; http://www.cnn.com
/2013/11/03/world/asia/shanghai-marriage-market/

3 http://www.guinnessworldrecords.com/world-records/longest
-kiss

4 http://articles.latimes.com/2012/jun/28/world/la-fg-india-gumshoe
-20120629; http://www.cracked.com/blog/the-6-most-terrifying
-dating-scenes-around-world/

5 https://www.researchgate.net/publication/230295149_Courtship_
Whistling_of_the_Mexican_Kickapoo_Indians; https://en
.wikipedia.org/wiki/Kickapoo_whistled_speech

6 https://matchmehappy.co.uk/blog/2013/12/01/evolution-dating-7
-courtship-customers-around-world-throughout-ages/; http://
amazing-notes.jimdo.com/the-most-unusual-traditions-courting
-for-a-girl/; http://bashny.net/t/en/103029

7 http://www.buzzfeed.com/readcommentbackwards/62-amazing
-fact-you-probably-didnt-know-that-will-dmjk#.kvN0V2kEkz

8 http://mentalfloss.com/article/28950/9-strange-courtship-rituals
-around-world; http://now100fm.cbslocal.com/2011/07/14/
how-sweaty-apples-used-to-be-a-sign-that-he-likes-you/

9 http://www.dailygazette.com/news/2013/apr/01/0402_dyngus_
wp/; http://www.ibtimes.com/what-dyngus-day-how-celebrate
-dyngus-day-anderson-cooper-pussy-willow-prince-video-1163457;
http://blog.cleveland.com/letters/2012/04/dyngus_day_has_
roots_in_spring.html

10 http://www.historicalnovels.info/Clisson-and-Eugenie.html

11 http://www.nytimes.com/2008/04/29/world/asia/29iht-sing
.1.12428974.html; http://www.cracked.com/blog/the-6-most
-terrifying-dating-scenes-around-world_p2/; https://app.sdn.sg/
AboutSDN.aspx

12 http://iloveuselessknowledge.com/2015/02/03/male-giraffes
-headbutt-female-giraffes-in-the-bladder-until-she-urinates-the
-male-giraffe-will-then/

13 http://www.toptenz.net/top-10-strange-courtship-rituals.php;
http://fathom.lib.uchicago.edu/1/777777190170/; http://www
.kingtutshop.com/freeinfo/Marrage-in-Ancient-Egypt.htm

14 http://www.dailymail.co.uk/femail/article-1036795/The-beauty
-prescription-Why-20-cent-attractive-think-are.html

15 http://www.salon.com/2015/02/14/love_is_like_cocaine_the_
remarkable_terrifying_neuroscience_of_romance/

Fast Facts: Invention Reinvention

1 http://mentalfloss.com/article/13092/bubble-wrap-was-originally
-supposed-be-wallpaper

2 http://www.huffingtonpost.com/entry/small-pocket-jeans-watches
-cowboys_us_56a7720ce4b0b87beec5eb5f

3 http://www.cheatsheet.com/personal-finance/5-inventions-that
-made-average-people-millionaires.html/?a=viewall

4 http://www.historyextra.com/article/ancient-greece/brief-history
-gestures-handshake-high-five

5 http://mentalfloss.com/article/29840/6-hugely-successful-products
-originally-invented-something-else

6 http://www.todayifoundout.com/index.php/2014/09/real-story
-potato-chip/

7 http://www.lifebuzz.com/strange-facts/3/

8 http://www.cnn.com/2010/LIVING/08/02/mf.cremation.ashes
.where.go/

YouTube Channel Remix

1 http://theweek.com/articles/464980/7-genetically-modified-animals
-that-glow-dark

2 http://www.expatica.com/nl/news/Herman-the-bull-heads-to
-greener-pastures_117386.html; http://www.telegraph.co.uk/news/
earth/agriculture/geneticmodification/8423536/Genetically
-modified-cows-produce-human-milk.html

3 http://www.dailymail.co.uk/news/article-2517137/The-Frankenfish
-GM-super-salmon-muscling-way-plate.html

4 http://news.bbc.co.uk/2/hi/asia-pacific/1780541.stm

5 http://www.healthline.com/health-news/tech-oxitec-mosquitoes
-dengue-fever-032213

6 https://www.sciencedaily.com/terms/dolly_the_sheep.htm; http://
www.independent.co.uk/life-style/health-and-families/health-news
/breakthrough-in-human-cloning-raises-hopes-for-treatment-of
-parkinsons-and-heart-disease-8617731.html

7 http://www.drugs.com/illicit/devils-breath.html

8 https://drugs-forum.com/forum/showwiki.php?title=DIPT

9 http://www.snopes.com/crime/warnings/jenkem.asp

10 http://hereandnow.wbur.org/2015/01/07/sugar-health-research

11 http://www.vpxsports.com/article-detail/drugs/dnp-the-most
-effective-and-dangerous-drug-for-fat-loss

12 http://imgur.com/gallery/73hUi

13 http://www.opioids.com/etorphine/immobilon.html; http://www
.savingrhinos.org/2012/03/05/m99-veterinary-drug-is-a-killer-in
-the-hands-of-unscrupulous-individuals/17799

14 http://www.bbc.com/news/magazine-27203322; http://www
.laweekly.com/news/ayahuasca-can-change-your-life-as-long-as
-youre-willing-to-puke-your-guts-out-4137305

15 http://www.drugs.com/illicit/krokodil.html

The Most Painful Pastimes on Earth

1 http://www.travelchannel.com/interests/outdoors-and-adventure/
articles/extreme-competitions; http://www.olimpickgames.com/
shin-kicking/; http://www.mirror.co.uk/news/weird-news/
most-bizarre-sport-ever-check-5803085; https://www.cayman

compass.com/2012/06/08/olympicks-celebrates-400-years-of
-history/

2 http://juneauempire.com/stories/072510/sta_683050556.shtml#
.VcJd3TBViko; http://www.weio.org/the_games.php

3 http://www.majorleagueeating.com/; http://time.com/2954614/
competitive-eating-health-risks/

4 http://www.npr.org/sections/monkeysee/2011/08/15/139642487/
okay-seriously-what-is-hillbilly-handfishin-glad-you-asked; http://
www.smithsonianmag.com/travel/hand-fishing-for-swamp
-monsters-70857913/?no-ist

5 http://www.herballove.com/case-studies/penile-weightlifting
-most-destructive-practice-penis; http://www.cosmopolitan.com/
sex-love/news/a35142/i-used-a-penis-weight-and-it-was-weird/;
http://believe-or-not.blogspot.com/2009/02/penis-strength
-competetion.html

6 https://en.wikipedia.org/wiki/Self-flagellation; http://news.bbc
.co.uk/2/hi/uk_news/magazine/8375174.stm

7 http://www.geekweek.com/2010/03/wrestling-gators-for-sport
.html; http://www.thecarpetbagger.org/2013/09/alligator-theater
.html

8 http://www.worldstarhiphop.com/videos/video.php?v=wshh5h2U
rkRCs9R2iet5; http://www.newworldencyclopedia.org/entry/
Snake_charming; http://www.dailymail.co.uk/news/article
-2972350/Pucker-Malaysian-snake-charmer-kisses-venomous
-snake-species-killed-father-TV-World-s-Talented.html

9 http://www.nerverush.com/sports-that-will-get-you-hurt-yikes/;
http://www.wingsuitfly.com/proximity-flying/4579414707; https://
en.wikipedia.org/wiki/Wingsuit_flying

10 http://espn.go.com/sports/endurance/story/_/id/13490557/
endurance-sports-lewis-kent-caitlin-judd-win-beer-mile-world
-classic-canada-takes-team-crown

Special Section: Japan Blows My Mind

1 http://www.openculture.com/2015/04/hoshi-a-short-film-on-the
-1300-year-old-hotel-run-by-the-same-family-for-46-generations
.html; http://www.gizmag.com/worlds-oldest-hotel-hoshi-japan/
13017/

2 https://en.wikipedia.org/wiki/Pinky_swear; http://english.stack
exchange.com/questions/125205/what-is-the-origin-of-the-phrase
-pinky-promise

3 http://www.whereintokyo.com/dbinx/animalcafe.html; http://www
.tofugu.com/travel/owl-cafe-fukuro-no-mise/

4 http://www.catholictradition.org/Mary/akita.htm

5 http://unscriptedmind.com/lala-the-shopping-penguin/#more-195;
https://www.youtube.com/watch?v=LcpcMxmLtCQ

6 http://www.dezeen.com/2014/08/15/akihiro-mizuuchi-chocolate
-lego-bricks/; http://www.thisiscolossal.com/2014/08/functional
-chocolate-legos-by-akihiro-mizuuchi/

7 http://www.thefactsite.com/2011/07/top-100-random-funny-facts
.html/4

8 http://www.odditycentral.com/travel/japans-okinawa-island-the
-healthiest-place-on-earth.html; http://www.okicent.org/study.html

9 http://www.cinemablend.com/television/Japanese-Game-Show
-Lets-Bears-Attack-People-Inside-Box-73177.html

10 http://www.themeparkreview.com/parks/photo.php?pageid=
100&linkid=1010

11 http://listverse.com/2014/02/24/10-amazing-legends-of-ninjas
-from-history/

12 http://www.independent.co.uk/news/world/asia/nagasaki
-anniversary-meet-tsutomu-yamaguchi-the-man-who-survived
-both-hiroshima-and-nagasaki-10447342.html

Ten Crazy Real-World Doppelgängers

1 http://dictionary.reference.com/browse/doppelganger?s=t

2 http://humansarefree.com/2013/12/the-amazing-connections
-between-inaca.html

3 http://www.aluxurytravelblog.com/2013/10/16/the-fake-city-of
-paris-in-china/; http://whenonearth.net/11-fake-european-towns
-landmarks-made-china/

4 http://mashable.com/2015/07/23/kepler-452b-earth-like-planet/;
http://www.cnn.com/2015/07/23/us/feat-nasa-kepler-planet
-discovery/

5 http://www.purpleclover.com/life-reimagined/1039-celebrities

-and-their-historical-twins/item/general-douglas-and-bruce-willis/;
http://www.businessinsider.com/check-out-these-celebrities
-and-their-ridiculous-historical-dopplegangers-2012-8?op=1;
https://en.wikipedia.org/wiki/Douglas_MacArthur

6 http://www.carbonated.tv/viral/these-two-girls-look-exactly-alike
-but-arent-even-related

7 https://en.wikipedia.org/wiki/Nephele; http://www.theoi.com/
Nymphe/NympheNephele1.html

8 https://en.wikipedia.org/wiki/Doppelgänger; http://www.egyptian
myths.net/mythgreek.htm

9 http://www.nytimes.com/1997/02/11/opinion/that-shiba-inu-in
-the-window.html; http://imgur.com/gallery/tfdbM; http://dogtime
.com/dog-breeds/shiba-inu

10 http://www.jockbio.com/Bios/Yao/YaoMing_bio.html; https://en
.wikipedia.org/wiki/Achilles; http://mythagora.com/bios/achilles
.html

11 http://dictionary.reference.com/browse/homonym; https://www
.spellingcity.com/homophones-and-homonyms.html

12 http://www.slate.com/articles/life/food/2012/09/tasting_like_
chicken_its_evolutionary_origins_.html; http://stephenwildish
.tumblr.com/post/41428989761/friday-project-it-tastes-like-chicken
-my-first; http://www.huffingtonpost.com/2013/02/07/exotic
-meats-tastes-chicken_n_2630622.html

Real Chinese Superstitions and Fake Canadian Superstitions

1 http://www.theworldofchinese.com/2013/01/the-5-dos-and-donts
-of-chinese-superstition/; http://audreymagazine.com/top-10
-most-outrageous-asian-superstitions/

2 http://randomwire.com/green-hat-a-no-no/; http://kotaku.com
/5936487/the-adulterous-shame-of-green-hats

3 http://www.theworldofchinese.com/2013/01/the-5-dos-and-donts
-of-chinese-superstition/

4 https://popculture.knoji.com/15-top-chinese-superstitions/

5 http://pregnant.sg/articles/common-chinese-pregnancy-taboos/;
http://www.echinacities.com/news/Bad-Luck-in-China-Avoid
-These-Superstitions-if-You-Can

6   http://papers.ssrn.com/sol3/papers.cfm?abstract_id=2434882
7   http://www.cloud9living.com/blog/dont-give-gift-death-chinese
    -gift-giving-101/
8   http://www.chinatownconnection.com/chinese-superstitions.htm
9   http://www.history.com/news/fireworks-vibrant-history
10 http://gohongkong.about.com/od/hongkongfestivals/tp/CNY
    superstition.htm
11 http://nowiknow.com/panda-diplomacy/
12 https://books.google.com/books?id=9Ka5BwAAQBAJ&pg=PA10&lpg
    =PA10&dq=if+a+line+of+chinese+people+walked+by+single+file&
    source=bl&ots=2D2zeAeDD0&sig=a4rQakEpovlYH-pR_Zz79eOOd
    1w&hl=en&sa=X&ved=0ahUKEwjv2c-YuuTLAhVEUBQKHY
    -JD9YQ6AEIRTAG#v=onepage&q=if%20a%20line%20of%20
    chinese%20people%20walked%20by%20single%20file&f=false

Fast Facts: More Powerful Than You Think

1   http://thenextweb.com/google/2012/08/28/fun-fact-one-google
    -search-uses-computing-power-entire-apollo-space-mission/#gref
2   http://www.economist.com/node/5571582
3   http://www.livescience.com/6040-brute-force-humans-punch.html;
    http://www.enchantedlearning.com/subjects/sharks/anatomy/
    Digestion.shtml
4   http://www.unisci.com/stories/20022/0523024.htm
5   http://dykn.com/your-stomach-acid-is-strong-enough-to-dissolve
    -razor-blades/
6   http://animals.mom.me/creature-sense-smell-3339.html; http://
    natgeotv.com/uk/casey-and-brutus-grizzly-encounters/facts
7   http://uselessfacts.net/page/57/
8   http://www.theanimalfiles.com/amazing_animals/amazing_animals
    .html
9   http://www.dictionary.com/slideshows/ough#thorough
10 http://www.washingtonpost.com/news/morning-mix/wp/2015/02
    /18/scientists-have-discovered-natures-newest-strongest-material
    -and-it-comes-from-a-sea-snail/

Historical Wizards and Their SWAG Rankings

1 https://en.wikipedia.org/wiki/Abe_no_Seimei; http://coolinteresting
   stuff.com/the-true-story-of-abe-no-seimei; http://listverse.
   com/2014/09/06/10-of-historys-most-fascinating-sorcerers/

2 http://www.firstworldwar.com/bio/rasputin.htm; https://en
   .wikipedia.org/wiki/Grigori_Rasputin

3 https://en.wikipedia.org/wiki/Edward_Kelley; http://www
   .alchemylab.com/kellydee.htm; http://www.crystalinks.com/
   philosopherstone.html; http://www.occultopedia.com/d/dee.htm

4 http://www.chabad.org/library/article_cdo/aid/111877/jewish/
   Rabbi-Judah-Loew-The-Maharal-of-Prague.htm; http://www.jewish
   mag.com/114mag/golem/golem.htm; http://matzav.com/the-maharal
   -of-prague-ztl-on-his-402nd-yahrtzeit-tomorrow-18-elul/

5 http://listverse.com/2014/09/06/10-of-historys-most-fascinating
   -sorcerers/; http://marblehead.wickedlocal.com/article/20140218/
   News/140216159; https://books.google.com/books?id=A0ZWWmd
   AlUgC&pg=PA419&lpg=PA419&dq=%22magician+of+marblehead

6 https://roadtrippers.com/stories/mistress-marie-laveau-the-voodoo
   -queen-of-new-orleans?lat=40.80972&lng=-96.67528&z=5; http://
   oldnolajournal.blogspot.com/2009/08/marie-laveau-voodoo-queen
   .html; http://www.themystica.com/mystica/articles/l/laveau_marie
   .html

7 http://www.nostradamus.org/; http://www.businessinsider.com/
   predictions-of-nostradamus-2011-12?op=1

8 http://www.omniglot.com/writing/magi.htm; http://www.the
   mystica.com/mystica/articles/p/paracelsus.html; http://www
   .alchemylab.com/paracelsus.htm; http://www.wonderslist.com/
   top-10-real-life-wizards-world/

9 https://knowledgeguild.wordpress.com/tower-of-london/; http://
   www.theguardian.com/artanddesign/jonathanjonesblog/2010/
   apr/12/hew-draper-tower-of-london-graffiti

10 http://www.rampantscotland.com/famous/blfamwizard.htm;
   http://www.philipcoppens.com/michaelscott.html; http://www
   .scotsman.com/news/scottish-wizard-who-tutored-the-pope-1
   -466356

Fast Facts: Word!

1 http://www.thefreedictionary.com/Overmorrow
2 http://www.nova969.com.au/station/national/viral-fix/article/mind-blowing-random-facts
3 http://www.to-hawaii.com/hawaiian-language.php
4 http://www.rinkworks.com/words/numbers.shtml
5 http://discovermagazine.com/2007/may/20-things-you-didnt-know-about-pencils
6 http://thoughtcatalog.com/bobby-viner/2013/07/30-weird-facts-most-people-dont-know/
7 http://www.oxforddictionaries.com/us/definition/american_english/sahara-desert
8 http://uselessfacts.net/page/7/
9 http://www.thefreedictionary.com/tittle
10 http://magoosh.com/toefl/2015/toefl-speaking-pronouncing-ough/
11 Ibid.
12 http://www.armaghplanet.com/blog/top-20-awesome-facts-about-space.html
13 http://blog.oxforddictionaries.com/word-of-the-year-faq/
14 http://mentalfloss.com/article/48657/20-words-we-owe-william-shakespeare
15 http://www.etymonline.com/index.php?term=u
16 http://www.nosweatshakespeare.com/blog/hip-hop-shakespeare/

YouTube Channel Remix

1 http://www.rantlifestyle.com/2014/09/28/15-urban-legends-that-turned-out-to-be-true/; http://abcnews.go.com/US/skeleton-found-chimney-27-years-man-disappeared/story?id=14169501
2 http://www.rantlifestyle.com/2014/09/28/15-urban-legends-that-turned-out-to-be-true/; http://www.dailymail.co.uk/news/article-1257330/Lifting-lid-macabre-history-buried-alive.html
3 http://usnews.nbcnews.com/_news/2012/03/09/10620190-inspired-by-weekend-at-bernies-two-denver-men-sentenced-in-corpse-case; http://www.thetoptens.com/urban-legends/
4 http://www.thetoptens.com/urban-legends/
5 Ibid.

6 Ibid.

7 Ibid; http://www.nbcnews.com/id/24889337/ns/world_news
   -weird_news/t/homeless-woman-lived-mans-closet-year/

8 http://www.thetoptens.com/urban-legends/; http://murderpedia
   .org/male.B/b1/bundy-ted.htm

9 http://www.rantlifestyle.com/2014/09/28/15-urban-legends-that
   -turned-out-to-be-true/

10 http://www.thetoptens.com/urban-legends/; http://www.rantlife
    style.com/2014/09/28/15-urban-legends-that-turned-out-to-be
    -true/

Special Section: The "Worst Pet on the Planet" Tournament

1 http://www.adfg.alaska.gov/index.cfm%3Fadfg%3Dlivewith
   .aggressivemoose

2 http://www.womansday.com/health-fitness/womens-health/
   a2532/8-things-you-didnt-know-about-mosquitoes-119183/

3 http://www.businessinsider.com/castoreum-used-in-food-and
   -perfume-2013-10

4 http://www.conservationinstitute.org/top-10-dangerous-animals
   -in-the-world/

5 http://www.feathersfinsandfur.com/penguins-as-pets-or-not/;
   https://www.youtube.com/watch?v=FCeCTv9xCks

6 http://thegoldfishtank.com/goldfish-facts/; http://www.tankterrors
   .com/top-10-fish-you-should-never-buy-for-your-aquarium/

7 http://www.boldsky.com/home-n-garden/pet-care/2012/aggressive
   -fish-aquarium-190412.html

8 https://www.nwf.org/Wildlife/Wildlife-Library/Amphibians
   -Reptiles-and-Fish/Sea-Turtles/Green-Sea-Turtle.aspx

9 http://www.centerforgreatapes.org/treatment-apes/apes-pets/;
   http://www.pbs.org/wnet/humanspark/blog/spark-blog-the-science
   -behind-why-chimps-are-not-pets/201/

10 http://www.bobcatsmt.com/pdfs/Guide.pdf; http://animals
    .nationalgeographic.com/animals/mammals/lynx/

11 http://www.theage.com.au/national/education/voice/why-arent
    -koalas-suitable-as-pets-20140708-3bkk1.html

12 http://mypetfox.com/post/5307400847/a-final-word-on-fox
    -ownership

13 http://www.huffingtonpost.com/2012/05/22/harry-potter-fans
    -abandoned-owls-england_n_1537056.html
14 http://www.livescience.com/23090-crows-grudges-brains.html
15 http://healthypets.mercola.com/sites/healthypets/archive/
    2015/05/16/raccoons-as-pets.aspx
16 https://www.reddit.com/r/BatFacts/comments/33v53u/bats_
    make_terrible_pets/; http://exoticpets.about.com/od/choosing
    anexoticpet/tp/TopTenAnimalsThatShouldNotBeKeptAsPets
    .htm
17 http://small-pets.lovetoknow.com/choosing-small-pet/are-sloths
    -good-pets; http://animals.nationalgeographic.com/animals/
    mammals/three-toed-sloth/
18 http://www.brainjet.com/random/3116/13-exotic-pets-you-totally
    -want-but-cant-have#page=3; http://www.peteducation.com/article
    .cfm?c=11+2072&aid=3349; https://en.wikipedia.org/wiki/Ferret
19 http://www.symmetrymagazine.org/article/april-2014/ten-things
    -you-might-not-know-about-particle-accelerators
20 http://www.humanesociety.org/issues/exotic_pets/facts/dangerous
    -exotic-pets-constrictor-snakes.html?referrer=https://www.google
    .com/
21 http://www.petmd.com/exotic/pet_lover/evr_ex_pg_fast_facts

Silly Robots

1 http://world.honda.com/ASIMO/; http://www.cnet.com/videos/
    hondas-asimo-robot-shows-off-new-moves/
2 https://www.youtube.com/watch?v=hMnk7lh9M3o
3 http://deepmind.com/; http://www.forbes.com/sites/paulrodgers/
    2015/02/28/googles-deepmind-masters-atari-games/
4 http://www.therobotbutler.com/; http://mashable.com/2014/11/06/
    robot-butler-brandspeak/
5 https://www.youtube.com/watch?v=NXWOiEzQ89A; http://www
    .roboticstrends.com/photo/the_best_robots_of_ces_2015/1
6 http://www.poweruptoys.com/; https://www.kickstarter.com/
    projects/393053146/powerup-30-smartphone-controlled-paper
    -airplane
7 http://www.techinsider.io/janken-robots-wins-rock-paper-scissors

-every-time-2015-9; http://www.nydailynews.com/news/national/
9-robots-completely-useless-human-race-article-1.2267299; http://
www.k2.t.u-tokyo.ac.jp/fusion/Janken/index-e.html

8　http://www.theverge.com/2014/3/11/5496284/this-is-what-robot
-strippers-look-like; http://www.huffingtonpost.com/2014/03/13/
robotic-pole-dancers_n_4951754.html

9　http://www.motoman.com/index.php; http://blog.robotiq.com/the
-most-useless-but-still-really-nice-robot-applications

10　https://en.wikipedia.org/wiki/Dolphins_-_Spy_in_the_Pod; http://
www.huffingtonpost.com/2014/02/10/robot-animals_n_4733672
.html

Real-Life Animal Avengers!

1　http://www.kidzworld.com/article/25704-top-5-animal-heroes;
http://survivor-story.com/dolphins-saved-boys-life/; http://www
.eurocbc.org/page158.html

2　http://old.post-gazette.com/regionstate/19981010pig2.asp; http://
old.post-gazette.com/neigh_west/20020409lulu0409p1.asp

3　https://www.youtube.com/watch?v=9JzjV2xS794; http://rojothe
llama.com/meet-the-animals/napoleon-the-alpaca/

4　http://www.huffingtonpost.com/2012/04/04/robert-biggs-bear
-mountain-lion-attack-hoax_n_1402801.html; http://www
.huffingtonpost.com/2012/03/29/bear-saves-man-from-mountain
-lion_n_1388219.html

5　https://en.wikipedia.org/wiki/Binti_Jua; https://www.youtube.com
/watch?v=1TqEU3VtUeM

6　http://animalheroes.livejournal.com/; http://www.animaltalk.us/
tuk-the-polar-bear-saved-kitten/

7　https://en.wikipedia.org/wiki/APOPO

8　http://nypost.com/2014/11/02/3-animals-who-saved-human
-children/; http://www.animalliberationfront.com/Philosophy/
Morality/Speciesism/2ParrotWarningStories.htm; http://www
.telegraph.co.uk/news/worldnews/northamerica/usa/5048970/
Parrot-saved-todlers-life-with-warning.html

9　http://news.bbc.co.uk/2/hi/africa/4116778.stm; http://www
.buzzfeed.com/chelseamarshall/the-most-heroic-animals-in-history

#.xb871MQEm; http://www.foxnews.com/story/2005/06/21/
lions-save-african-girl-from-abductors.html

10 http://thestir.cafemom.com/healthy_living/134344/amazing_cat_
saves_womans_life; http://www.dailymail.co.uk/health/article
-2090635/Breast-cancer—My-kitten-alerted-cancer-kept-jumping
-breast.html

11 https://www.youtube.com/watch?v=LU8DDYz68kM

12 https://en.wikipedia.org/wiki/Lockjaw_and_the_Pet_Avengers;
http://www.comicvine.com/throg/4005-30596/

Fast Facts: All in the Family

1 http://www.huffingtonpost.com/2013/06/06/facebook-divorce
-linked-i_n_3399727.html

2 http://www.today.com/news/seeing-double-twin-marries-twin-they
-have-identical-twin-boys-1B7999284

3 http://www.latimes.com/local/obituaries/la-me-wayne-allwine21
-2009may21-story.html

4 http://www.wildflowers-and-weeds.com/Plant_Families/Rosaceae
.htm

5 http://news.bbc.co.uk/2/hi/middle_east/4642916.stm

6 http://www.niihauheritage.org/niihau_history.htm

7 http://mic.com/articles/86047/four-of-the-world-s-most-iconic
-rappers-went-to-high-school-together

8 http://www.mlive.com/news/grand-rapids/index.ssf/2009/05/
reunion_of_man_birth_mother_wh.html

Exceptional Child Prodigies

1 https://www.youtube.com/watch?v=8_eAkdtYay4; http://
all-that-is-interesting.com/worlds-most-talented-kids/2; http://
mymultiplesclerosis.co.uk/ec/akrit-jaswal-child-surgeon/; http://
www.quora.com/Smart-People/Where-is-Akrit-Pran-Jaswal-What
-has-he-been-doing-lately

2 http://www.gardenofpraise.com/art20.htm; https://www.youtube
.com/watch?v=bVxk7b9HigM; http://www.nytimes.com/1989/
07/16/arts/gallery-view-a-painting-prodigy-but-still-a-child.html;
https://en.wikipedia.org/wiki/Wang_Yani

3   https://www.youtube.com/watch?v=Yi_5xbd5xdE

4   https://en.wikipedia.org/wiki/Bobby_Fischer; http://www.chess
     games.com/perl/chess.pl?tid=54397; http://www.psmag.com/books
     -and-culture/a-psychological-autopsy-of-bobby-fischer-25959;
     https://en.wikipedia.org/wiki/The_Game_of_the_Century_(chess)

5   http://glennvance.com/2007/07/12/galusha-pennypacker-the
     -youngest-brigadier-general-in-the-us-army/; http://www.history
     net.com/who-was-the-youngest-civil-war-general.htm

6   http://www.npr.org/sections/thetwo-way/2012/05/31/154050046/
     youngest-speller-is-out-of-the-bee-tripped-up-by-ingluvies

7   http://www.popsicle.com/campaigns/popsicle-story/; http://www
     .todayifoundout.com/index.php/2011/08/the-popsicle-was-invented
     -by-an-11-year-old/; http://www.history.com/news/hungry-history/
     frozen-history-the-story-of-the-popsicle

8   https://www.youtube.com/watch?v=tf2J8hktI5Y

9   https://en.wikipedia.org/wiki/Grammy_Award_records#Youngest
     _winners

10   http://www.answers.com/Q/Who_invented_the_first_scooter;
     https://books.google.com/books?id=s3zCkSd_MPYC&pg=PA46&lp
     g=PA46&dq=walter+lines+1897+scooter&source=bl&ots=BDBuuy
     96ow&sig=m2pPteUo1DnI7KUJLB3r7R3MO2o&hl=en&sa=X&ved
     =0ahUKEwjgoYTtx-nLAhWlmIMKHeFkBqsQ6AEIITAB#v=one
     page&q=walter%20lines%201897%20scooter&f=false

11   http://lilpoison.com/

12   http://www.ipl.org/div/mushist/clas/mozart.html

13   http://mom.me/home/3937-best-kid-inventions-history/item/
     trampoline/

14   http://www.bbc.co.uk/history/historic_figures/henry_vi_king
     .shtml

YouTube Channel Remix

1   http://www.cfhtlens.org/public/what-gravitational-lensing

2   http://skepdic.com/pareidol.html; http://listverse.com/2013/06
     /09/10-astounding-examples-of-pareidolia-in-outer-space/

3   http://www.cnet.com/news/mars-curiosity-rover-sings-happy
     -birthday-to-itself/#!

4   http://www.nasa.gov/mission_pages/galex/20070815/v.html

5 http://www.space.com/19748-hypervelocity-stars-milky-way.html
6 http://www.universetoday.com/120353/what-makes-mars-sunsets -different-from-earths/
7 http://www.sciencebits.com/Gliese581
8 http://www.solstation.com/stars2/castor6.htm
9 http://www.howitworksdaily.com/do-metals-fuse-together-in-space/
10 http://asd.gsfc.nasa.gov/blueshift/index.php/2013/07/12/jasons -blog-next-stop-diamond-planets/
11 https://en.wikipedia.org/wiki/Himiko_(Lyman-alpha_blob)
12 https://www.ras.org.uk/news-and-press/224-news-2013/2212 -astronomers-discover-the-largest-structure-in-the-universe
13 http://phenomena.nationalgeographic.com/2014/03/13/a-guide-to -lonely-planets-in-the-galaxy/
14 http://tycho.usno.navy.mil/leapsec.html
15 http://www.universetoday.com/14280/how-long-is-a-day-on -mercury/
16 http://money.cnn.com/2014/09/25/news/india-mars-cost/

Fan Facts from Around and About the Globe

1 http://www.nortrade.com/sectors/articles/norways-introduction -of-salmon-sushi-to-japan/
2 http://eilat-petra.com/facts-about-petra-jordan/; http://www.calvin .edu/petra/about/
3 http://www.belgische-bieren.be/bieren
4 http://www.tellows.co.uk/countryprefix/7/Russia
5 https://en.m.wikipedia.org/wiki/Wadi-us-Salaam
6 http://www.irishcentral.com/culture/craic/top-ten-little-known -facts-about-ireland-ahead-of-the-gathering-2013-173265331 -237761001.html
7 http://www.insidermonkey.com/blog/11-countries-that-consume -the-most-milk-348978/; http://www.worldatlas.com/articles/top -10-coffee-consuming-nations.html
8 http://wafflesatnoon.com/russia-bigger-than-pluto/
9 http://o.canada.com/entertainment/50-insane-facts-about-canada -we-bet-you-didnt-know
10 http://theflama.com/fascinating-facts-peru

11 http://www.mirror.co.uk/news/world-news/botox-capital-of-the
    -world-welcome-to-westport-1595294
12 http://www.irishcentral.com/culture/craic/20-interesting-facts
    -about-the-Irish-and-Ireland-PHOTOS.html
13 https://www.cdr.wisc.edu/mastercheesemaker/requirements
14 http://www.weekendnotes.com/interesting-facts-about-netherlands/
15 https://en.m.wikipedia.org/wiki/Hungry_Jack%27s?repost#History
    _of_.22Burger_King.22_in_Australia
16 http://www.hawkesbaynz.com/index.php/see-do/maori-culture/
    places/the-longest-place-name-in-the-world
17 https://www.google.co.in/search?q=samoa+to+american+samoa+
    distance&oq=samoa+to+american+samoa+distance&aqs=chrome
    .69i57.12713j0j7&sourceid=chrome&es_sm=93&ie=UTF-8
18 http://gawker.com/5683326/worlds-biggest-jesus-statue-is-finally
    -complete
19 http://www.universetoday.com/27064/what-is-the-largest-desert
    -on-earth/

Facts About My Favorite Things

1 http://www.shortlist.com/entertainment/films/15-things-you
    -(probably)-didnt-know-about-get-him-to-the-greek
2 http://www.imdb.com/name/nm1214289/#actor
3 http://movies.about.com/od/gethimtothegreek/a/jonah-hill-get
    -him-greek_2.htm
4 http://www.gamespot.com/gallery/16-amazing-facts-about-the
    -legend-of-zelda-that-yo/2900-28/; https://en.wikipedia.org/wiki/
    Princess_Zelda; http://uproxx.com/gammasquad/2014/05/15
    -fascinating-facts-you-may-not-know-about-the-legend-of-zelda/
5 http://www.slate.com/articles/life/food/2012/12/robert_c_baker_
    the_man_who_invented_chicken_nuggets.html
6 http://www.buzzfeed.com/robinedds/things-you-probably-didnt
    -know-about-the-simpsons#.dkBW7Zzd3s; http://www.thefactsite
    .com/2012/02/30-facts-about-homer-simpson.html
7 http://www.cnn.com/2014/12/17/showbiz/tv/the-simpsons-25
    -years-feat/
8 http://nobert-bermosa.blogspot.com/2011/09/60-entertaining
    -and-interesting-facts.html; http://mentalfloss.com/article/29962

/11-little-known-facts-about-frank-sinatra; http://onpoint.wbur
.org/2010/11/02/fun-facts-frank-sinatra

Fan Fact Favorites

1 http://premierhandling.com/where-are-twizzlers-made/
2 http://www.buzzfeed.com/daves4/one-sentence-facts#.fubN162eG
3 https://en.m.wikipedia.org/wiki/Nasal_cycle
4 http://snowbrains.com/brain-post-how-far-does-the-average
   -human-walk-in-a-lifetime/
5 http://ultimateclassicrock.com/john-lennon-ended-beatles-at-
   disney/
6 http://www.fearof.net/fear-of-ducks-phobia-anatidaephobia/
7 http://www.lifebuzz.com/strange-facts/
8 https://en.m.wikipedia.org/wiki/Pandora%27s_box
9 http://www.lego.com/en-us/aboutus/lego-group/the_lego_history
10 http://www.edgartownschool.org/uploads/files/david_faber/
   The%20amazing%20human%20body!.ppt
11 https://twitter.com/uberfacts/status/492101105065951232
12 http://mentalfloss.com/article/52275/65-amazing-facts-will-blow
   -your-mind
13 Ibid.
14 http://www.factslides.com/s-Math
15 https://www.google.co.uk/webhp?sourceid=chrome-instant&rlz=
   1C1CHWA_enGB612GB612&ion=1&espv=2&es_th=1&ie=UTF-8#q
   =what%20is%20scotland%27s%20national%20animal&es_th=1
16 http://m.mentalfloss.com/article.php?id=52275
17 https://en.wikipedia.org/wiki/Laser; http://acronyms.thefree
   dictionary.com/LASER
18 http://gizmodo.com/there-are-more-ways-to-arrange-a-deck-of
   -cards-than-ato-1553612843
19 http://www.gpb.org/blogs/the-daily-jog/2013/03/25/what-you
   -may-not-know-about-mr-rogers; https://www.youtube.com/
   watch?v=4Xck2ByutMg

INDEX

Palmer, Walter J., 43–44
pandas, 109
panties, 17
paper airplane enabler, 152–53
Paracelsus, 120
Paradise, Dick, 45
pareidolia, 176–77
Paris, 98–99
Parker, Richard, 44
parrot, 161–62
Payet, Pascal, 27
Peck, Charles, 130
pencils, 124
penguins, 137
  Lala, 90
penile weight lifting, 82
Penney, James Cash, 42
Pennypacker, Galusha, 172–73
Persia, 18
Peru, 186
Petra, 185
pets, 135–46
Pharrell, 189
phone calls from the dead,
  130
pigs, 30
  in battles, 165
  genetically modified, 73
  LuLu, 158
  potbellied, 144, 158
Pink, 189
pinky swears, 88–89
planets, 181
  Earth, 19, 99, 179, 182

55 Cancri e, 180
Gliese 581c, 179
Mars, 19, 176, 177, 178,
  182
Mercury, 182
rogue, 181–82
Poe, Edgar Allan, 44
Poland, 188
polar bear, 160–61
pole-dancing robot, 154–55
policeman, killer, 132–33
Popsicles, 173–74
potassium, 76
power and strength, 111–12
PowerUp 3.0, 152–53
Predator Shield, 92
pregnant women, 107–8
Presley, Elvis, 21
prisons:
  escapes from, 25–29
  most brutal, 30–32
proximity flying, 84

quasars, 181
quietly dead guy, 129

raccoons, 141, 143, 145
rai stones, 7–8
Rasputin, Grigori, 115
Rat Pack, 192
rats, 144
  in toilet, 130–32